UNDERSTANDING ARCHITECTURE
A GUIDE TO ARCHITECTURAL STYLES

UNDERSTANDING ARCHITECTURE
A GUIDE TO ARCHITECTURAL STYLES

LINDSAY MATTINSON

This Amber edition first published in 2019

Copyright © 2019 Amber Books Ltd

All rights reserved. No part of this publication may be reproduced, stored in a retrieval system, or transmitted in any form or by any means, electronic, mechanical, photocopying, recording, or otherwise, without prior written permission of the copyright holder.

Published by
Amber Books Ltd
United House
North Road
London
N7 9DP
United Kingdom
www.amberbooks.co.uk
Instagram: amberbooksltd
Facebook: www.facebook.com/amberbooks
Twitter: @amberbooks

ISBN: 978-1-78274-748-2

Project Editor: Sarah Uttridge
Design: Jerry Williams and Mark Batley
Picture Research: Terry Forshaw
Additional Research: Jasmine Hayden and Sophie Hardy of Mattinson Associates Ltd.

Printed in China

CONTENTS

Introduction	6
Chapter 1: Architecture of the Ancient World	8
Chapter 2: Architecture of the Middle Ages	28
Chapter 3: 15th–16th-Century Architecture	58
Chapter 4: 17th-Century Architecture	80
Chapter 5: 18th-Century Architecture	100
Chapter 6: 19th-Century Architecture	126
Chapter 7: 20th-Century Architecture	148
Chapter 8: Masters of the 20th Century	178
Chapter 9: 21st-Century Architecture	206
Glossary	220
Index	221

The Cathedral of Brasília is one of the city's most famous and instantly recognizable buildings.

INTRODUCTION

For millennia, the major works of the built world were created by kings, emperors and religious leaders to express their status and to glorify their deities. The tour through architectural history in this book is dominated at first by the still-existing structures built by these powerful individuals. Many of these were splendid, and of course expensive, buildings of great significance that were constructed to withstand the centuries. Their 'architects' were actually artists, sculptors, scientists, masons and master builders who typically never saw a building completed in their lifetime. The 16th century saw the emergence of the architect as an independent professional solely in charge of the design and delivery of the building, led by luminaries such as Andrea Palladio. Today, architects study for several years and work with myriad specialists to design complex buildings that may take up to five years to complete.

The first examples we consider in this book illustrate how early architecture was monumental in scale yet often simplistic in form, as a result of basic engineering and the limited structural integrity of building materials. Progressing through history, we see that engineering skills improved, new building materials were adopted and architecture took on new forms.

Architecture can be classified into styles that run through history, each influencing the next. These styles bleed into one another and overlap through the centuries; as one style established itself in one part of the world and later spread elsewhere, new styles were arising at the point of origin. In this book we have arranged the styles chronologically, with each chapter featuring a style and a building that illustrates it, outlining the main characteristics of the style and how it relates to the built example. Some buildings in the book do not fall perfectly into the timespan of the chapter, but stretch beyond it; however, they are true examples of the style of architecture to which they are attributed.

This book is not just a description of the history of architecture relative to individual buildings. It also enables the reader to view the progress through time of technology, building methods and the expanding realm of what it is possible to achieve. As the world has become more technologically advanced, design boundaries have been pushed and ever-more outstanding buildings have been produced. This has happened throughout history, and today we are achieving what would have been considered impossible in the past. The future for architecture remains extremely exciting.

ANCIENT ARCHITECTURE
El Castillo at Chichen Itza, Mexico, built between the 8th and 12th centuries AD, is an example of monumental architecture on a grand scale.

MODERN ARCHITECTURE
The Guggenheim Museum, Bilbao, by Frank O. Gehry (1997) illustrates how modern contemporary architecture has progressed with the use of new materials and technology, allowing building forms to take on new and exciting shapes and making anything possible in the built form.

KEY ARCHITECTURAL STYLES OF THE ANCIENT WORLD (4500 BC – 400 AD)

SUMERIAN (4500 BC – 2000 BC)
Early monumental architecture in Mesopotamia (in the area of the Tigris and Euphrates rivers) is thought to have originated with the development of an understanding of mathematics, celestial and solar configurations, and the invention of writing. Conscious attempts at architectural design were made in the construction of Sumerian buildings; however, builders and architects did not fully understand how buildings might remain standing if they had vast internal spaces, resulting in buildings being very solid and the walls often featuring buttress-like projections.

ANCIENT EGYPTIAN (3250 BC – 400 AD)
Ancient Egyptian architecture is an expression of one of the most influential civilizations throughout history. A vast array of structures and great architectural monuments were built, including pyramids, tombs, temples and palaces. These buildings were highly engineered and architecturally complex and could only have happened with the organization of huge skilled and unskilled workforces. Buildings other than pyramids were highly decorated with carved relief imagery, stand-alone statues and hieroglyphs describing historic stories.

MESOAMERICAN (2000 BC – 1500 AD)
Mesoamerican architecture was produced by pre-Columbian civilizations, in a region stretching from Mexico through Belize, Guatemala, El Salvador, Honduras, Nicaragua and northern Costa Rica. It is best known for its public, ceremonial and urban monumental structures. These cultures had an advanced understanding of astronomy and engineering, incorporating symbolism into their city planning and architectural design and aligning their structures accordingly.

ASSYRIAN (1800 BC – 600 BC)
The militaristic Assyrian empire in Mesopotamia used art and architecture to display its power. Assyrian aggression resulted in a rapidly expanding empire, which at its peak spread from Cyprus in the west to the Persian Gulf in the east, giving builders access to many resources, including stone and iron. The development of iron tools led to the creation of enormous rectangular palaces based on stone slab foundation walls (orthostats) decorated with elaborate relief carvings depicting war.

ANCIENT GREEK (700 BC – 300 AD)
Ancient Greek architecture is renowned for its tall, fluted columns, defined architectural orders, intricate detail, symmetry, harmony, perspective and proportion. Temples were conceived as a structural entity within the landscape, situated on high ground, creating an impression of elegance and dominance from afar. Architectural style was defined in three orders: Doric, Ionic and Corinthian, identified by the style of column. Ancient Greek architecture included temples, public buildings and large theatres with sophisticated acoustics cut into hillsides.

ANCIENT ROMAN (700 BC – 400 AD)
Ancient Roman architecture adopted and reshaped the language of Classical Greek architecture, embracing the three Classical orders and also exploring and pushing the limits of materials and support engineering. The Romans mastered the arch and vault and perfected concrete as a building material, bringing a new dimension to their buildings that the Greeks never had. Therefore, for the first time in history, form, height and internally unobstructed space could be fully explored.

ARCHITECTURE OF THE ANCIENT WORLD

The development of architecture in the ancient world was closely aligned with the scientific, sociological and political advancements that happened almost simultaneously in different regions. The key aspirations of these early civilizations were to allow the powerful to consolidate their control over a population and to bring them closer to the gods.

The earliest writing, cuneiform, took place in the earliest Sumerian cities, as a means to keep track of the increased complexity of city life and who owned what property. Ancient Egypt was one of the earliest civilizations to make use of papyrus and ink, as well as to make significant advances in construction. The ability to accurately record and pass on building processes allowed for the replication of structures. The architect of the earliest monumental stone building is believed to have been Vizier Imhotep, architect to Pharaoh Djoser in the 27th century BC. This structure was the Pyramid of Djoser, which was itself a development of the mastaba, a flat-roofed, rectangular structure with inward-sloping sides, constructed out of mud bricks. There is still debate as to how it was possible to construct the pyramids with little more than human strength, but it is interesting to note that similar processes must have been employed for the pyramids built by the Nubians in Sudan, who were influenced by their neighbours in ancient Egypt, and the far distant cultures of Mesoamerica. The ancient Romans drew on the expertise of their predecessors, which they studied closely, then took architectural and engineering skill and style to heights and complexities never seen before.

MAYA CARVING
A stone carving found in the Great Ball Court at Chichen Itza, Mexico, depicts the decapitation of a ballgame player with a skull-marked ball at the centre.

SUMERIAN 4500 BC – 2000 BC

- Among the earliest **permanent** structures
- Mud **bricks** with reed binder
- **Platform temples** with huge staircases
- Exterior walls ornamented with recesses and alternating **buttresses**

ZIGGURAT OF UR

Architect: Unknown, built by King Ur-Nammu
Construction started: c.2050–2030 BC
Construction completed: c.2030–1980 BC
Construction materials: Mud brick with burnt brick facing
Height/Area: Over 30m (98ft) and 2880sq m (31,000sq ft)
Location: Nasiriyah, Iraq

The Ziggurat of Ur, one of the best preserved Sumerian structures, was built to honour the moon god Nanna. Although its step-pyramid structure was massive, the actual height is not definitely known because only the bottom of the structure survived and was then renovated. The original ziggurat crumbled to ruins by the 6th century BC, partly due to attacks by the Elamites, and only the foundations remained when King Nabonidus restored it. After many attempts at excavating the ruins, they were extensively excavated in the 1920s and 1930s by Sir Leonard Woolley. In the 1980s, Saddam Hussein ordered a partial reconstruction, with part of the main façade and the main staircase being rebuilt. As these renovations aimed to show its original appearance, the Ziggurat of Ur we see today is not the same as the excavated structure.

The Ziggurat is thought to have originally been made of successively smaller platforms of mud brick covered with burnt brick to protect the core of the structure from the elements, supported by recesses and alternating buttresses. The small rectangular openings on the façade are not windows but apertures to let moisture escape the structure. The grand stairway faces the first rays of the summer sun following the celestial line, providing evidence of advanced astronomical knowledge. Some believe ziggurats were dedicated to a celestial god and provided their earthly home; others believe that the building at the summit was merely an observatory. If this is the case, the ziggurat could also have been a centre for innovation, study and progressive thinking.

BRICK STAIRWAY
The reconstructed brick stairway alongside the partially reconstructed façade would have provided access to the stacked platforms and temple-type structure located at the summit.

ANCIENT EGYPTIAN 3250 BC – 400 AD

- **Monumental** stone temples built in limestone, granite and sandstone
- Large **stone pillars** supporting heavy stone temple roofs
- **Relief carvings** of pharaohs, hieroglyphs and gods

LUXOR TEMPLE

Architect: Unknown, built by Amenhotep III (1390 BC–1352 BC); Tutankhamun (1332 BC–1323 BC); Horemheb (1319 BC–1292 BC); Ramses II (1279 BC–1213 BC); and Alexander the Great (332 BC–323 BC)

Construction started: c.1390 BC

Construction completed: c.1213 BC

Construction materials: Nubian sandstone temple and surrounding wall in mud brick

Area: 10,480sq m (112,810sq ft)

Location: Luxor, Egypt

Luxor Temple was probably built over an earlier temple. It was constructed by more than 2000 slaves under Amenhotep III and later completed and added to by Ramses II, other pharaohs, Alexander the Great and the Romans. Luxor Temple is one of the best-preserved ancient Egyptian monuments, with extensive structural elements and relief carvings still intact. The temple complex consists of four main structures connected in a low processional row. The complex is approached along a 3-km (2-mile) route flanked by 1400 stone-carved sphinxes with Ramses II heads. The entrance to the complex is marked by a *pylon*, or 65-m-high (213ft) gate, decorated with battle scenes, and is guarded by two 15-m-high (50ft) seated statues of Ramses II carved in granite and four ruined standing statues. Two 25-m-high (82ft) obelisks carved in red granite were also located here, although one now sits in the Place de la Concorde in Paris.

The outer courtyard of Ramses II is lined with 74 papyrus columns resembling bunches of tied reeds with closed-bud capitals. A colonnade connecting this area with another outer courtyard is formed of 16-m-high (52ft) open-flower papyrus columns supporting huge lintel stone blocks. This courtyard, built by Amenhotep III, has double rows of papyrus columns on three sides. Behind it lies the Hypostyle Hall, originally a stone-roofed structure supported by many rows of columns and lintels and only intended for the high priest or pharaoh. The overall scale of the Luxor Temple complex and the detail found on the ornate relief carvings and statues represents a time of great progress in architectural history.

OPEN-FLOWER PAPYRUS COLUMNS

The colonnade of Amenhotep III has seven pairs of tall open-flower papyrus columns that support huge lintel blocks made of stone, and links the two outer courtyards.

BUD CAPITALS (LEFT)
Papyrus columns with bud capitals holding ornately carved stone lintels in the courtyard of Ramses II display a high quality of craftsmanship and carved symbolism. This forecourt was never intended to hold a roof and remains an open space.

RAMSES II COLOSSI (RIGHT)
In the southern part of the courtyard of Ramses II there are a number of standing colossi of the pharaoh in varying states of ruin.

HEAD OF RAMSES II (BELOW)
Ramses II was the third pharaoh of the 19th Dynasty of Egypt and was the most celebrated, and perhaps the most powerful, pharaoh of the New Kingdom.

MESOAMERICAN 2000 BC – 1500 AD

- **Limestone** carved with stone tools
- **Mortar** and stucco of crushed, burnt and mixed limestone
- **Post** and **lintel** support for high slanted roofs in wood, thatch or stone

CHICHEN ITZA

Architect: Unknown, built by Mayans
Construction started: c.600 AD
Construction completed: c.1200 AD
Construction materials: Limestone and stucco
Area: 10sq km (4sq miles)
Location: Yucatan State, Mexico

The city of Chichen Itza is renowned for its striking architecture. The city illustrates how monumental construction was used to support a rigid hierarchical society. It is rich in monumental architecture and sculpture that emphasizes the militarism of the culture, with imagery of jaguars, eagles and feathered serpents. Probably a capital city ruling over neighbouring areas, Chichen Itza was one of the great Mesoamerican city complexes and its sophisticated architecture reflected this status.

For example, El Castillo is a pyramid structure with nine levels, which may symbolize the nine layers of the underworld. At the bottom of one ramp are two stone carvings of feathered serpent heads. Four steep and narrow staircases run across the tiers and climb directly to the square platform and shrine at the top, which consists of two narrow rooms with a steeply corbel-vaulted roof sitting above the tree canopy allowing for unobstructed views. The architecture of this pyramid has a close connection to astronomy, with shadows from the setting sun on autumn and spring equinoxes running up and down the central staircase. Using more columns and broader lintels resulted in wider galleries and larger interior spaces, providing a structure wider than previously seen.

The city had several ball courts, including the Great Ball Court, where players hit a heavy ball through a stone ring on either end wall and it is believed that one captain was sacrificed to the gods at the end of the game. The Las Monjas is covered in extensive carvings of the rain god Chac. Together with the Temple of Warriors, and skull racks where enemy heads where displayed, the entire city centre was steeped in a culture of militarism which called for monumental architecture.

LAS MONJAS
The intricately carved eastern wing of the building is considered one of the most beautiful and best-preserved buildings of Chichen Itza. Young women chosen to serve as priestesses, and later sacrificed, are thought to have lived here.

ASSYRIAN 1800 BC – 600 BC

- Square-based, **tower**-like structures
- Massive **fortified walls**
- **Wood**, stone, clay brick and metal used
- **Vivid colours**, painted decorations, enamelled tiles

PALACE OF SARGON AT KHORSABAD

Architect: Unknown, built by King Sargon II
Construction started: c.713 BC
Construction completed: 706 BC
Construction materials: Wood, mud bricks, limestone and precious metals
Area: 2.88sq km (1.11sq miles)
Location: Khorsabad, Nineveh Province, Iraqs

The Palace of Sargon at Khorsabad was irreparably damaged in 2015 by ISIL, who destroyed most of the remaining parts of the ancient monument. Fortunately, the complex had already been documented and a few sculptural elements from the palace were already housed in museums and universities, keeping some of its history intact.

Until this event there were remains of a very thick 12m-high (40ft) wall built from blocks of stone, carved with images offering detailed descriptions of how the palace may have looked. The fortress complex was built on a high terrace with massive walls holding 157 towers to protect it. The fortress was rectangular in plan, with a stone foundation rising above ground level to form an orthostat base with seven openings to enter the city. The entrances were great round arches flanked by square towers with overhanging parapets and battlements. Carved figures of Lamassu (a deity shown as a winged bull with a human head) weighing around 36 tonnes (35 tons) each guarded the entrances, providing a formidable presence. This fortress held the emperor's palace, ziggurat and temples of the main gods. Temples were built within the palace rectangle, allowing the emperor to exercise greater control over the priests and giving him more prominence than the gods, thus altering the cultural hierarchy. Sargon planned his palace in monumental proportions to match that of his vast empire. Walls were decorated with long rows of relief carvings depicting war scenes and festival processions. Sargon died in battle before completing his capital. His son succeeded him but moved the capital elsewhere. The palace was finally abandoned a century later when the Assyrian empire fell.

LAMASSU CARVING
These stone lamassu figures, with a human head, the body of a bull or a lion, and bird wings, were believed to have been set on each side of the main entry to the Palace of Sargon as guardians. They were intended as a political symbol of Assyrian superiority, lying in wait ready for enemy attack.

ANCIENT GREEK 700 BC – 300 AD

- **Columns** gave order, strength and balance
- **Doric**, **Ionic** or **Corinthian** columns and capitals
- **Lintel** to carry the roof structure
- **Frieze** above the lintel with historic relief carvings

THE ACROPOLIS, ATHENS

Architects: Ictinus, Mnesicles and Callicrates and sculptor Phidias
Construction started: c.460 BC
Construction completed: c.406 BC
Construction materials: Marble and limestone
Area: 30,400sq m (327,200sq ft)
Location: Athens, Greece

The Acropolis is deemed one of the most significant architectural monuments of the ancient world. It established the basis of architectural order and influenced most, if not all, architecture that followed. The current buildings were built on the site of an ancient citadel, on a rocky outcrop in the heart of Athens. The temple complex, largely constructed on the orders of the statesman Pericles, was built above the city of Athens to create a lasting monument to the goddess Athena and to glorify the cultural and political achievements of the people of Athens.

The four main buildings of the Acropolis were the Propylaia, the Parthenon, the Erechtheion, and the Temple of Athena Nike. The Propylaia is the ornate entranceway into the temple complex, while the Parthenon was the most famous temple, originally housing a large gold and ivory statue of Athena. The temple is based on the proportions of the Doric order; a notable feature is that the building elements were designed to create a false perspective (using curved and tapered, rather than straight, lines) so the building would be viewed as perfectly proportioned from afar. The Erechtheion was considered the most sacred area of the complex and served Athena as well as other gods and heroes. It is on the northern side of the site where the original temple destroyed by the Persians was located. The side chapel is held up by carved freestanding female statues called caryatids. The Temple of Athena Nike is of the Ionic order and was constructed to protect the most vulnerable access point to the Acropolis. The Acropolis and its famous Parthenon provide a perfect example of ancient Greek order, symmetry and proportion.

IONIC ORDER
Marble fluted columns and scroll capitals are seen on the Temple of Athena Nike. Only the remnants of the pediment can be seen.

THE PARTHENON (RIGHT)
The Parthenon temple, dedicated to the goddess Athena, is the most famous marble structure on the Acropolis. At either end it features a double row of eight columns in the Doric order.

CARYATIDS (BELOW)
The south porch of the Erechtheion consists of intricate designs to accommodate the uneven landscape. The caryatids, or female form columns, are replicas. Most of the originals are in the Acropolis Museum; one is in the British Museum in London.

ANCIENT ROMAN 700 BC – 400 AD

- Post and lintel became **arched** construction
- **Arches** made larger and with higher spans
- Triumphal **arches** and structures
- **Roads** and **aqueducts**

THE COLOSSEUM, ROME

Architect: Unknown, built by Emperors Vespasian and Titus
Construction started: 72 AD
Construction completed: 80 AD
Construction materials: Travertine limestone and tuff for pillars and radial walls, clay floor and wall tiles, and concrete for vaults
Height/Area: 48m (157ft) and 20,000sq m (215,300sq ft)
Location: Rome, Italy

The Colosseum amphitheatre is the largest building of ancient Rome and paved the way for the modern-day stadium. It held up to 75,000 spectators and allowed for the efficient circulation of people. The exterior was built using the Classical style of superposed orders adopted from ancient Greece, with varying styles of column arranged vertically from the simplest at the bottom of the structure to the most elaborate at the top. Romans used vaulted construction to build freestanding venue seating, allowing these buildings to be erected anywhere.

The Colosseum is oval in shape and mostly constructed of three floors of arcades: on the ground floor there are Tuscan engaged columns (a Roman version of the Doric column embedded in the walls); on the first floor Ionic order semi-columns; and on the second floor Corinthian engaged columns. The final storey has no arches and is divided by flat composite Corinthian columns with alternate rectangular windows. There are 80 stacked arches per floor and these become successively smaller at each floor, allowing for taller construction.

The walls of the Colosseum were constructed from blocks of travertine limestone secured with iron grips, while cast concrete vaults supported the vast seating areas. The arena floor was made of timber planks that could be drawn back to allow gladiators and animals to rise from the undercroft. The sheer scale of this structure, and its advanced engineering, proves that Ancient Roman architecture was the beginning of a more sophisticated era, exploring technology to build higher, larger and more magnificently.

TRAVERTINE ARCHES
The travertine arches of the outer walls were made from blocks set without mortar and held together with 272 tonnes (268 tons) of iron grip clamps. These grips were removed over time, leaving holes between the blocks of stone.

INTERIOR STRUCTURE
The interior of the Colosseum includes a basement area, or *hypogeum*, which held the wooden staging area for gladiatorial and other events, and the cages for the wild animals used in some shows.

KEY ARCHITECTURAL STYLES OF THE MIDDLE AGES (476–1492)

PERSIAN/ISLAMIC (610–900)
Influenced by Roman, Byzantine and Persian civilizations, Islamic rulers also developed the style of the newly conquered Byzantine Empire, from where they sourced many craftsmen. Islamic architecture makes use of specific ornamentation of elaborately geometric patterns and calligraphic inscriptions.

BYZANTINE (400–1500)
Byzantine architecture was influenced by Classical architecture and Eastern spires and domes. It was the building style of Constantinople, formerly Byzantium and now Istanbul. The most distinctive feature was the domed roof resting on a square base with a symmetrical central plan.

MOORISH (650–1500)
Moorish architecture of North Africa and the Iberian Peninsula was based on Islamic architecture. Influences were widespread, from regions including North Africa, Western Europe and Syria. The Moors added plumbing and irrigation systems, resulting in a hybrid of cultural, engineering and architectural styles.

MEDIEVAL RUS' (1000–1250)
The architecture of the medieval Kievan Rus' state established itself after the adoption of Christianity and was influenced by Byzantium. A new style then emerged in Russian church architecture with strong Romanesque elements.

ROMANESQUE (1040–1170)
Romanesque architecture was influenced by Roman and Byzantine architecture and was the first pan-European style to emerge since the Roman Empire. Buildings show regional characteristics with frequently repetitive symmetrical ideas. The appearance is of simplicity, proportion and order.

NORMAN (1070–1250)
Norman architecture describes notably large English stone buildings constructed in the Romanesque style by the ruling Normans. The Norman style developed in Normandy and England simultaneously alongside Gothic architecture but became much more distinctive in England.

MUDÉJAR (1125–1600)
The Mudéjar style of post-Moorish Iberia had no new shapes or structures but a mix of Islamic and medieval Christian elements resulting from a convergence of Moorish and European cultures. It is characterized by red-brick-patterned relief work, particularly for bell towers, achieving strikingly decorative results.

GOTHIC (1130–1550)
Gothic architecture marks a shift from the earlier 'dumpy' Romanesque style to a lighter, impressively tall form with a pointed quality. Delicate in execution yet structurally robust, this style can appear almost fantastical as it seemingly soars towards the heavens.

MING CHINA (1368–1644)
Classical Chinese buildings emphasize breadth over height. They feature an enclosed, heavy platform and wooden frame structure with wooden infill walls. Typical of this style are large, heavy tiled roofs that 'float' over supporting vertical walls.

PERPENDICULAR GOTHIC (1350–1550)
Perpendicular Gothic is an English version of Gothic architecture. It is more economical in its design compared to previous styles, with a lower pitched roof and more daylight internally. Main features are strong vertical lines, intricate tracery on immense windows and heavy internal panelling.

ARCHITECTURE OF THE MIDDLE AGES

The fall of the Roman Empire disrupted the culture of the early European Middle Ages. Organized religion arose in part to fill the resulting power vacuum, becoming a key influencer in the lives of the general population and giving rise to some of Europe and the Islamic World's most dramatic and groundbreaking buildings.

After the collapse of the Roman Empire, Europe witnessed grappling for power, in-fighting and segregation. Wealth wasn't abundant, resulting in the construction of very few large, monumental buildings. For example, under Norman rule almost all land in England was owned by the king, who gifted it to his subjects. Most surviving Norman buildings are castles or churches. As prosperity increased, the Romanesque style grew and the grandeur of the Roman Empire was replicated across the continent, growing up simultaneously but also spread by travellers and the Church. Meanwhile, the autocratic Ming dynasty in China had succeeded the Yuan (Mongol) dynasty (1271–1368), finding expression in refined and imposing architecture, and Europeans began to travel to Asia to find the newest spices, as well as silks, crafts, precious stones and metals.

From the 7th century, Islam spread from the Middle East across North Africa and into Asia and Europe, carrying along with it its distinctive architectural styles, which saw unique syncritism in the Moorish and Mudéjar styles of Iberia and the Norman-Arab architecture of Sicily. By the end of the Middle Ages, trade, communication and advances in transport had brought about great change, both socially and architecturally.

NORWICH CATHEDRAL NAVE
Norwich Cathedral has an extremely long nave consisting of 14 bays, each terminating at ceiling level with an intricately ribbed vault.

PERSIAN/ISLAMIC 610–900

- **Rich** patterns and symmetrical silhouettes
- **Byzantine** domes
- Pointed, ogee, horseshoe and **multifoil arches**
- **Exterior** ornamental detail with patterned brickwork

THE TOMB OF THE SAMANIDS, BUKHARA

Architect: Unknown, built by Ismail Samani
Construction started: 892
Construction completed: 943
Construction materials: Kiln-dried bricks
Height: 10.6m (35ft)
Location: Bukhara, Uzbekistan

This mausoleum is the only surviving monument of the Persian Samanid dynasty that ruled in Central Asia in the ninth and tenth centuries. It is one of the oldest examples of Islamic architecture in Central Asia and marks a new phase in the development of Central Asian and Persian architecture. While the overall structure is based on the ancient tradition of the kiln-dried brickwork Persian fire temples, it has a higher standard of decorative detail, achieved by introducing Islamic designs from Arabia and Persia and combining these with native Zoroastrian religious motifs.

The mausoleum's simple yet brilliant design is composed of a semi-spherical dome on a cube with four façades sloping slightly inwards as they rise, supported by four internal arches upon which the dome sits. All the façades are identical, with a three-quarter domed corner column. There's an upper armature and a central entrance with a visible horizontal dividing line, all typical of Islamic architecture in the Middle Ages. Horizontal, vertical and diagonal patterns cover the walls, along with details in the shape of rosettes. All elements in the mausoleum are based on squares and diagonals, forming geometrically digressive lines. The same unification is seen in the architectural forms and kiln-dried brickwork inside the building. At a high level along each side are ten small windows providing ventilation for the interior.

The architectural design of the mausoleum is entirely unique. It owes much to pre-Islamic architecture yet also anticipates the emergence of a new architectural style within comparatively small dimensions and leaves one with a feeling of moving from one world to another.

MAUSOLEUM INTERIOR
A geometric timber lattice entrance door held within a pointed arch and surrounded by patterned brickwork allows mottled 'quiet' light into the inner sanctum of the space.

BYZANTINE 400–1500

- **Centralized** church plan
- **Awe-inspiring** column and arch interiors
- Large **pendentive domes** enabling a square-shaped base
- **Richly luminous** gold stained glass and mosaics

HAGIA SOPHIA, ISTANBUL

Architects: Isidore of Miletus and Anthemius of Tralles
Construction started: 532
Construction completed: 537
Construction materials: Brick and mortar
Height: 55.6m (182ft)
Location: Istanbul, Turkey

Hagia Sophia is arguably the greatest surviving example of Byzantine architecture and is undoubtedly a magnificent architectural achievement. It is one of the only known buildings to have served three denominations or religions: Eastern Orthodox and Catholic Christianity, and Sunni Islam. Hagia Sophia can be seen from miles away due to its sheer scale, oversized buttresses, monolithic domes and far-reaching minarets, symbolizing the cultural hybrid that makes Byzantine architecture so rich and awe-inspiring. Until the 15th century, no building incorporated a floor space so vast under one roof. The structure is a series of domes of varying scale. The magnificent central dome sits over the nave 55.6m (182ft) from floor level and rests on an arcade of 40 arched windows. At the eastern and western entrances arched openings are extended by half domes of identical diameter to the central dome. They are carried on smaller semi-domes over semi-circular recesses, building up a series of domed elements creating a vast rectangular interior crowned by a 76.2m (250ft) diameter central dome.

Extensive golden glass mosaics stud the interior to form a glittering canopy overhead, each one set at a slightly different angle to reflect light. Carved decorative panels in imported Italian and Egyptian marble cover the walls and 140 purple porphyry and green marble columns hold up the semi-domes, their capitals finely carved in acanthus and palm tree leaves with monograms of emperors. The splendid figurative mosaics were added in the ninth century, although many of these have been lost. The few that remain are unique in that they cover most of the history of Byzantium under one roof. Hagia Sophia is Byzantine on an immense scale.

FINELY CARVED CAPITALS
Purple porphyry and green marble columns from Egypt and Italy terminate in capitals finely carved with acanthus and palm tree leaves and inlaid monograms of the emperors.

PENDENTIVE DOME (RIGHT)
Hagia Sophia has an impressively vast pendentive domed roof and exquisite luminosity achieved by using gold mosaic to form a glittering canopy, reflecting light from the windows.

MIHRAB (BELOW)
The *mihrab* is situated in an ornate apse. This niche indicates the *qibla* (or direction of Mecca) to be used by Imams to lead prayers. It is ornamented with tiles and verses from the Koran while adjacent are Christian mosaics and stained-glass decorations. The juxtaposition of Islamic and Christian elements is profound.

MOORISH 650–1500

- Decorative geometric and **calligraphic inscriptions**
- Ornamented **pillars**, horseshoe and scalloped multifoil arches
- *Muqarnas* (decoratively carved honeycombed vaulting)
- Large **courtyards** with water

ALHAMBRA, GRANADA

Architect: Unknown, built under Muhammed I, Yusuf I and Muhammed V
Construction started: 1238
Construction completed: 1358
Construction materials: Tapia (rammed earth) and stone
Area: 142,000sq m (1,530,000sq ft)
Location: Granada, Andalusia, Spain

The Alhambra (Red Fort) was built as a fortified complex for the Nasrid rulers of Granada. The complex is recognizably different from other medieval palaces due to the high degree of complexity in its planning, exquisite execution of its decorative work, and its well-considered gardens and ingenious water features.

The exterior walls of the fortress have a stark functional aesthetic, hiding the jewel of Moorish detail contained within its walls. Three original royal palaces lie within the walls. The Comares Palace, with its elaborate carved stucco façade, is set back from the Court of the Myrtles and pool. The Comares Tower contains a throne room holding the most varied architectural elements at Alhambra. Double-arched windows frame views and arched lattice-like windows set high in the walls flood daylight into the interiors. Intricately detailed tiles laid in geometric patterns adorn walls and beautiful carved stucco motifs are arranged in alternate patterns to provide curved and calligraphic designs. The Palace of the Lions consists of arched verandas wrapped around a central courtyard of which the focal point is a complex hydraulic fountain supported by twelve stone lions. The arched verandas are made from intricate stucco carvings supported on a series of elegant columns. A series of arches lead up to vaulted *muqarnas* ceilings and large domed side rooms that are lavishly covered with star-shaped stucco in *muqarnas* form. The Partal Palace is the oldest palace structure at the Alhambra, featuring an intricately carved geometric patterned portico that addresses a large reflection pool. Together these palaces and their interconnecting structures within the walls of the Alhambra form an exquisite example of Moorish architecture.

COMARES INTERIOR
Windows in the Comares Tower are formed from double arches supported by miniature pillars with arched lattice-like infill. Secondary windows are set high in the walls to flood daylight into the interior.

ALHAMBRA COMPLEX
In this view of the Alhambra complex taken from the Mirador de San Nicolas, the large Comares Tower can be seen in the forefront, the Palace of the Lions located behind, the 16th-century Palace of Charles V to the right and the Partal Palace to the extreme left.

MEDIEVAL RUS' 1000–1250

- **Romanesque** influence: thick walls, small narrow windows, helmeted cupolas
- **Carved** double-recessed niches, in rhythm on façade
- Coloured painted **frescoes**
- Almost **square churches** with one dome

CATHEDRAL OF SAINT DEMETRIUS, VLADIMIR

Architect: Unknown, built under order of Grand Prince Vsevolod III
Construction started: 1194
Construction completed: 1197
Construction materials: Local white limestone blocks
Height: 30m (98ft)
Location: Vladimir, Russia

The Cathedral of St Demetrius is a royal church. It is one-domed, four-pillared and square in form, with three internal naves. Originally it was connected to the Grand Prince's palace but now stands alone. It was one of the most beautiful and most distinctive cathedrals in the medieval state of Kievan Rus' and is famous for its intricate external white stone carvings. Artisans from the east and west worked on the relief carvings on the façade, which express many different influences. They show an eclectic and complex mix of saints with real and mythical animals, plant motifs, and geometric patterning, all indicating a contemporary philosophy of life. The carved façades are intended as one conceptual design to illustrate the perfection of the world, in line with the universal law of harmony. These carvings cover the upper half of the exterior walls above the arcade frieze and below the domed cupola in horizontal bands corresponding to the rows of white stone masonry.

Built using stone-faced rubble masonry, the cathedral is small and based on the proportions of the 'golden ratio', making it a truly balanced design providing visual equilibrium. The long, thin windows and relatively small doors are deeply recessed with extensive carved ornamentation, providing further shadow and interest on the façades. The building is refined and dignified yet shines with a simple, natural brilliance that makes it a remarkable piece of architecture. Originally the walls and vaults inside the cathedral were covered with beautiful frescoes of varying expertise, which may have been the work of Byzantine masters with the help of Russian pupils. These frescoes have only partially survived, along with a few carvings inside the cathedral.

CONCENTRIC ARCH
Multiple-columned and highly carved concentric arches create a recessed white limestone niche, providing dramatic decoration at the base level of the façade upon entry to the cathedral.

ROMANESQUE 1040–1170

- **Load-bearing** columns and ornamental pilasters
- Carved **capitals** with geometric patterns, floral images and mythical creatures
- **Semi-circular** arches with simple mouldings

LEANING TOWER OF PISA

Architects: Diotisalvi but also attributed to Guglielmo, Bonanno Pisano and Tommaso di Andrea Pisano
Construction started: 1173
Construction completed: 1372
Construction materials: White marble and stone
Height: 55.86m (183ft)
Location: Pisa, Italy

During the height of the Romanesque period, Pisan architects came up with the superb design of the marble Cathedral of Pisa, based on simplicity, proportion and order. It sits next to the Leaning Tower of Pisa and Pisa Baptistry and Cloister. The tower is actually a Romanesque campanile, or freestanding bell tower, located behind the Cathedral, and is famous for its unprecedented height, cylindrical shape and unintended tilt.

Construction of the Romanesque tower occurred in three stages over 200 years. The ground floor is a blind arcade articulated by engaged columns with Classical Corinthian capitals, coloured marble inserts and relief carvings typical of the Romanesque period. During construction of the second floor the tower began to sink due to insufficient foundations and poor subsoil conditions, halting its construction, which was only resumed a century later when the ground conditions had stabilized. Engineers decided to compensate for the tilt by building the upper arched galleries of the tower with one side taller than the other, resulting in a curved tower. The tower's exterior thick white marble and stone walls are made up of decorative arcading on each floor. Simple repetition of round arches and blind galleries form a beautiful relief lattice pattern climbing the height of the tower, while repeating arches and columns provide a depth to the detailing that creates a simple yet rich patterning on the tower typical of the Romanesque period. Thus, with the simplest of ideas and repetitive, regular and seemingly symmetrical resolution, the whole building becomes both intricate and interesting. The Leaning Tower of Pisa is a Romanesque masterpiece and very progressive for its time.

WHITE MARBLE RELIEF WORK
Stone capitals crowning each column are individually carved in relief with intricate geometric patterns, floral images, animals and mythical creatures, including two monkeys held in chains by an eagle shown here.

NORMAN 1070–1250

- **Massive proportions**, square towers and minimal ornamental decoration
- **Austere** and fortress-like
- Tiers of **round arches** rising one above the other
- **Larger** stained-glass windows

NORWICH CATHEDRAL

Architect: Unknown, built for Herbert de Losinga, Bishop of Norwich
Construction started: 1096
Construction completed: 1145
Construction materials: Flint and mortar faced with cream-coloured Caen limestone
Height: 96m (315ft)
Location: Norwich, United Kingdom

Norwich Cathedral, with its overwhelming scale, was one of the largest churches to be built in Europe in the Middle Ages. Its location near to the River Wensum was strategic in bringing in stone from Normandy to construct the cathedral.

Norwich Cathedral has an uncharacteristically long nave consisting of 14 bays, each terminating at ceiling level with an intricately ribbed vault. The eastern end terminates at the high altar in an apse with a covered walkway between two strangely shaped side chapels. These are based on two overlapping circles, allowing for a more streamlined altar orientation. The ground floor arcade runs through the nave, transepts and chancel. This forms the base for a further layer of sweeping arches making a first-storey blind arcade, followed by a second storey of arches with glass windows allowing clerestory light into the building. These sweeping arcades provide a dramatic and awe-inspiring ascent within the building. The internal ornamentation and carvings are minimal, with simple zigzags on arches and beautifully intricate ribbing. The tower is located directly over the intersection of the cruciform plan and topped with the second tallest spire in England, after Salisbury Cathedral. The cloisters that sit in the elbow of the nave and south transept are the second largest medieval cloisters in England. They enclose a large, not quite square, lawn area with eight double-arched corner openings and 38 triple-arched openings with scalloped arches, intricate tracery and slender pillars. Each arch is made up internally of a rib-vaulted ceiling with ornately carved and painted rib junctions (or 'bosses') providing a series of passageways that allude to the overall grandeur of the cathedral.

THE CLOISTER
The original cloister was destroyed in 1272 and rebuilding was only completed in 1430. Evidence of this is seen in the sudden change in design of the stone tracery on the open window arcades.

MUDÉJAR 1125–1600

- **Islamic influences** and repetitive rhythmic patterns
- Elaborate and sophisticated **geometrical** tilework, brickwork and plasterwork
- **Slanted** wooden ceilings supported by stone arches

SAN MARTIN TOWER, TERUEL

Architect: Unknown
Construction started: 1315
Construction completed: 1316
Construction materials: Brick and ceramic glaze
Height: Approx. 14.4m (47.2ft)
Location: Teruel, Aragon, northern Spain

The tower of the Church of San Martin is a square-based gate-tower with a cobbled street passing directly through its pointed barrel (or 'ogival') arch. This truly original architectural solution responded to a lack of building space and is found only in Teruel. Due to its height above the town, the tower was used as a belfry and watchtower, allowing for surveillance of the area, and is located close to the Daroca Gate that controlled access into the city. The tower consists of two concentric towers separated by a gap of 1m (3ft) with corridors and stairs leading through this gap up to the belfry – a style derived from the Islamic influence of Almohad minarets. The inner tower is finished in plaster mortar and the outer tower in red brickwork. There are three floors with three superposed rooms covered by a single pointed vault support. The top section of the tower contains the belfry, which reflects Christian influences.

The exterior of the tower displays all the delicacy and detail of Arabic decoration, although more developed than previously seen in Islamic architecture. The façades are broken up into differing decorated bands of design spanning horizontally up the façade. The ornamental brickwork sections are immensely complex and consist of angled brickwork alternating with highly glazed ceramic tiles. Brick mixtilinear arches (an arch whose inner edge consists of broken concave and convex curves), saw-tooth banding and geometric relief patterning are interspersed with ceramic tile inlays dyed green with copper oxide and white with tin plate, then glazed with lead, providing a luminous glaze that brings the façade to life. The tiles display a range of shapes: square and rhombic, plates and discs, herringbone treads, chevrons and graceful slender cylindrical columns and even eight-pointed stars.

CERAMIC AND BRICK PATTERNING
Red brick relief patterning in intricate geometric shapes is adorned with green and white ceramic checkerboard and star motifs and cut-outs.

GOTHIC 1130–1550

- **Flying** buttresses and sharp pointed spires
- Large expanses of **glass tracery** windows
- Pointed **arches** and ribbed vaults
- **Stone** structures with intricate sculptures and gargoyles

NOTRE-DAME CATHEDRAL, PARIS

Architect: Unknown, built under the orders of Maurice De Sully, Bishop of Paris
Construction started: 1163
Construction completed: 1345
Construction materials: Courville limestone, lead and iron
Height: Towers 68m (226ft) and spire 91.4m (300ft)
Location: Paris, France

Notre-Dame is considered one of the finest examples of French Gothic architecture and is distinguished for its size, antiquity and architectural interest. The western main façade is probably the finest and most characteristic in France. Although flying buttresses were developed in late antiquity, this was one of the earliest major buildings to incorporate flying buttresses as a means of supporting a vaulted roof. The buttresses enabled Gothic architecture to become lighter and taller, affording a greater aesthetic experience than before. The imposing west façade has three deeply recessed portals formed from pointed arches with successive encircling tiers and a central doorway split in half by a carved statue of Christ. A band of carved statues depicting the kings of France separates the base from the twin tower composition above. A beautiful 9.6m (31ft) diameter central rose window divided by stone mullions visually separates the tower forms and adds symmetry to the overall composition. The cathedral's three great rose windows retain their 13th-century glass and are regarded as one of the greatest masterpieces of Christian architecture. This façade is proportionately harmonious and simple yet complex. The eastern end of the cathedral presents whimsical qualities with very slender flying buttresses, allowing for the walls to become thinner and for the introduction of more glass.

The slim spire rises 91.4m (300ft) into the air, emphasizing the verticality of the style, while the carvings of mythical and grotesque gargoyle waterspouts provide a fantastical quality that firmly roots this building in Gothic architecture. The impressive interior leads one's eyes to the main altar along the ribbed nave, lined by an arcade of cylindrical columns with Corinthian-style capitals.

GARGOYLE
Grimacing stone gargoyles adorn the outer edges of the roofed areas of the cathedral, adding a mythical decorative quality to the functional waterspouts.

FLYING BUTTRESSES (ABOVE)
Flying buttresses were used both for aesthetic purposes and as a structural device to transfer loading from the vaulted roof to the ground, allowing stone walls to become thinner and more glass to be used.

CENTRAL NAVE (LEFT)
Columns lining the nave support the ribbed-vault roof structure through the triforium and clerestory, providing an inner open space with immense verticality and soaring proportions.

MING CHINA 1368–1644

- **Symmetrical** arrangement on a **central axis**
- A strong **horizontal emphasis**
- **Dougong** (wooden brackets) supporting heavy tiled roofs
- **Complex** roofs with overhanging eaves

THE FORBIDDEN CITY, BEIJING

Architects: Kuai Xiang, Nguyễn An and Cai Xin
Construction started: 1406
Construction completed: 1420
Construction materials: Timber logs, rammed earth, marble, baked 'golden' bricks and yellow glazed roof tiles
Area: 720,000sq m (7,750,000sq ft)
Location: Beijing, China

The Forbidden City was designed in a way that typifies traditional Chinese palatial architecture, with emphasis on articulation and bilateral symmetry to signify balance. As the complex was designed to be the centre of Beijing, this symmetry follows the north–south axis of the old city. It's laid out in a rectangle surrounded by a wall and moat, with the corners expressed by four towers. The imposing Meridian Gate at the southern entrance opens onto the Outer Court through which the Golden River runs, crossed by five white marble bridges. Towering above the Outer Court is the Hall of Supreme Harmony, the most iconic structure of the complex, which also houses the throne of the emperor. It is the largest building in the complex and one of the largest surviving wooden structures in China. The impressive column and beam structures are made from timber. Intricately engineered interlocking *dougong*, or wooden brackets, help to reduce the impact of earthquakes on the buildings. This allowed for separate infill wall panels that could be changed or reconfigured if necessary, resulting in a palace evolving on demand depending on the needs of each emperor. These panels were then adorned with richly painted panels to protect the underlying timber and to provide decoration.

Imperial paintings in buildings on the central axis and inside the main palaces include dragons to protect emperors and phoenixes to protect empresses. Ancillary decorations are based on geometric motifs and found on walls and doors of annexed pavilions and smaller rooms. The palace complex is a model of feudal Chinese architecture and represents the culmination of the art of this civilization.

STONE ARCHES
It is thought that the large stones used to build parts of the city were transported on sledges along frozen paths of wet ice.

GLAZED TILE ROOF (ABOVE)
Yellow glazed tiled roofs are rich in style and artistic value. They slope gradually in a concave fashion with deep overhangs to keep rainwater away from the timber and earthen structure below. These roofs carry magnificent, intricately carved and decorated ridge and hip tiles.

WATCH TOWERS (RIGHT)
The Forbidden City is laid out in a rectangle and is surrounded by a wall and moat. The corners of the city are decorated by four towers with intricate roofs featuring multiple ridges.

INTRICATE AND ORNATE CEILING (FAR RIGHT)
Coffered ceilings with intricate recessed panels and ornately carved cornicing painted in colourful patterns based on geometric motifs are found in smaller ancillary rooms. This type of decoration is generally found in palace complexes rather than 'civilian' houses.

PERPENDICULAR GOTHIC 1350–1550

- **Large windows**, slim stone mullions and linear tracery
- Magnificent **low pitch** open timber roofs
- **Panelled** decoration highlighting the perpendicular
- Light and elegant **fan vaulting**

KING'S COLLEGE CHAPEL, CAMBRIDGE

Architects: Reginald Ely, Simon Clerk and John Wastell (master masons), begun by Henry VI
Construction started: 1446
Construction completed: 1515
Construction materials: Yorkshire white magnesian and Northamptonshire oolitic limestone
Height: 29m (94ft)
Location: Cambridge, United Kingdom

King's College Chapel, within a college of the University of Cambridge, is one of the world's finest examples of late Perpendicular Gothic architecture and is full of Tudor symbolism. It's characterized by soaring vertical lines and large narrow-traceried windows filled with immense expanses of stained glass. There is more glass than stone in the side façades, allowing for a light-filled interior that previous styles had not been able to achieve.

The pitch of the roof is far lower than had been seen before and the resulting internal structure of fan vaulting is exceptional, being both the largest in Europe and so complex that it was an incredible architectural achievement for its time. The fans are divided up by a series of shallow ribs and, unlike earlier Gothic ribbed vaults, these ribs are decorative rather than structural. The vertically expressed fluted columns leading down the nave are decorated with carved Tudor motifs and coats of arms, and the strong vertical lines of the entire chapel even extend to the window tracery. Stained-glass windows run along each side of the entire length of the nave. The upper sections of these windows hold lace-like tracery and are filled with richly coloured stained-glass biblical stories. Pointed arches and flying buttresses are used to heighten and widen these windows, providing essential support and visual framing. Although an ornately carved wooden chancel screen and choir stalls were added later, King's College Chapel remains the finest example of Perpendicular Gothic architecture standing today.

FAN VAULTING
The magnificent limestone fan vaulting took three years to complete and was created by master mason John Wastell.

KEY ARCHITECTURAL STYLES OF THE 15TH AND 16TH CENTURIES

RENAISSANCE (1400–1600)
Renaissance architecture was a conscious progression from the ancient Classical orders. Order and proportion dominated and beauty was expressed through the translation of human proportion to built proportion. Internal space was organized using scale, form and geometry rather than intuition. The verticality and intricacy of Gothic architecture was abandoned in favour of simplicity and balanced proportions.

VERNACULAR TUDOR (1485–1603)
The Tudor period saw an increasing number of modest houses constructed within towns and the countryside as lifestyles improved. This English vernacular architecture is characterized by timber frame construction with solid ground floors in stone or brickwork and upper levels in decorative half-timbering with masonry or stucco between the timbers. The timber frame allowed for the creation of better internal space.

MANUELINE (1490–1550)
The Age of Discovery brought a great wealth of knowledge into Portugal as Portuguese explorers such as Vasco da Gama revealed new civilizations, resulting in an influx of foreigners. The arrival of new cultural and architectural influences led to a reinterpretation of Gothic and Renaissance styles to form the Manueline style (named after King Manuel I). Maritime influences were heavily referenced on buildings with carvings of navigational instruments, elements of the sea, naval motifs and details of newly discovered lands.

HIGH RENAISSANCE (1500–1525)
The High Renaissance witnessed the pinnacle of Classical simplicity and harmony, used with great confidence. This era is notable for the way it expressed the Classical orders in a contemporary manner, creating a new, simplified version. The central plan layout (taking Roman temples and the Pantheon as a precedent) was popular. Plan forms were based on rotational symmetry, resulting in circular, square and octagonal buildings.

MANNERISM (1525–1600)
Mannerism emerged during the late Renaissance and is characterized by sophistication, complexity and new ideas. This style explored the relationship between the solid and the spatial. It employed the Giant order, where tall pilasters reach up the entire façade of the building, resulting in more imaginative solutions free from the rigid order and rhythm previously used.

MIDDLE MUSCOVITE (1530–1630)
The 16th century saw Muscovite power begin to be expressed in a profusion of magnificent high-tented, multi-domed, red-brick structures. Each new building was larger and more ornately decorated than its predecessor. Large numbers of these buildings were constructed after Italian architects persuaded Muscovites to replace limestone with brick, arguing it was cheaper, lighter and easier to use.

ELIZABETHAN (1558–1603)
Before the reign of Elizabeth I, ecclesiastical buildings dominated, but Elizabethan architecture turned to great houses that reflected continental European influences from printed architectural texts, coupled with the detailing and materials traditionally used in England at the time. As a result, this era saw the birth of the aspirational 'prodigy house', or magnificent country house, using decoration derived from Mannerism with elements from medieval castles such as the busy roof line.

15TH–16TH-CENTURY ARCHITECTURE

The 14th century brought about a fundamental transformation of culture and saw the evolution of modern social norms not only across Europe, but all around the world. On the whole, societies saw a shift away from devout religion and saw a rise in secular culture, which resulted in the rise of domestic architecture.

Reform was widespread in Italy and saw the rise of individualism, allowing increased social mobility. This breakaway from traditional values required new rules. For the population, new-found secularism meant the beginning of a new world, which went hand in hand with a great flowering in architecture and art. In England, the Tudors, well known for running a country steeped in medieval tradition, embraced the momentum begun in Europe, and Henry VIII set about reducing the power of the Church. Grand royal palaces and country houses proliferated. Simultaneously, Portugal was prospering under Manuel I's reign (1495–1520), which saw the birth of Portugal's Age of Discovery and a new forward-thinking style of architecture. In the late 15th and early 16th centuries, the scientific advances of Copernicus and Galileo, and geographical discoveries by Magellan and Columbus, left Europe rattled. These challenges to the widely accepted canonical view brought about the realization that Europe was not the centre of the world and that the Earth was not the centre of the Universe. In the mid-16th century, Russia began to grow, gaining an area approximately the size of the Netherlands each year. Russian architecture found magnificent new forms.

PALAZZO DUCALE
The Hall of Mirrors is part of the Palazzo Ducale, in Mantua, Italy, built by the Gonzaga family between the 14th and 17th centuries.

RENAISSANCE 1400–1600

- Revival of **Classical orders** and use of pilasters, pediments, columns, arches, domes, cupolas and vaults
- Façade veneers in **Planar (flat) classicism**
- More decorative and **ornamental**

FLORENCE CATHEDRAL

Architects: Arnolfo di Cambio and Filippo Brunelleschi
Construction started: 1296
Construction completed: 1436
Construction materials: Brick, marble and sandstone
Height/Area: 114.5m (376ft) and 8300sq m (89,340sq ft)
Location: Florence, Italy

The basilica is one of Italy's largest churches and its dome is still the largest brick and mortar dome in the world. Both the dome and the front façade were design competitions at different times. The façades illustrate Planar classicism, where walls are decorated with Classical motifs including relief pilasters, pediments and blind arches that provide a two-dimensional green, white and red marble veneer. The cathedral's main entry façade was originally a collective work but was never completed. Following a much later design competition, it was replaced in 1887 by the heavily decorated masterpiece seen today.

Originally the dome was imagined as extremely tall in order to span the huge interior space, but the engineering knowledge to achieve this was lacking until Brunelleschi found a technical solution in 1407. He envisaged a drum and then designed the dome to fit it, building both Gothic and Renaissance elements into the structure. Based on a double shell of brickwork, the octagonal outer shell supported by ribs in a pointed arch profile refers to the Gothic style, and was used alongside the more up-to-date engineering of the self-supporting dome. Structural reinforcing was engineered from vertical marble ribs and horizontal sandstone rings connected with iron rods. These were supported by a timber structure tying the ribs together, allowing the structure to rise without collapsing. A herringbone brick pattern transferred the weight of the bricks to adjacent vertical ribs. The two brick shells were tied internally with arches, making a self-buttressed design that required no further external support to keep it in place. The aesthetic of the dome is magnificently Renaissance, yet still quietly refers to the Gothic structure.

ROSE WINDOW
The circular window with intricate stone mullions and tracery makes a striking statement over the main portico entrance to the cathedral and has its roots in Gothic architecture.

PLANAR CLASSICISM (ABOVE)
The cathedral's façades are true examples of Planar classicism, where walls are embellished with Classical motifs such as blind arches, pilasters and pediments of varying depth of relief to create a mulitfaceted impression.

BRONZE DOOR (RIGHT)
The central portal holds ornately carved bronze doors decorated with relief scenes from the life of the Madonna. A deeply recessed mosaic *lunette*, or half-moon shape, above the door is framed with highly decorative relief carvings.

INTERNAL DOME FRESCOES (FAR RIGHT)
Brunelleschi intended the interior of the dome to be in mosaic decoration to reflect light from the drum windows and lantern. However, this was not realized and it was instead painted with a representation of the Last Judgement by Vasari and Zuccari.

VERNACULAR TUDOR 1485–1603

- Timber **cruck frame**
- Thatch or slate **steeply pitched** gable roof
- Six-to-eight-pane **casement windows** in diamond leaded glass
- **Half-timbering** with masonry or stucco in between

ANNE HATHAWAY'S COTTAGE, STRATFORD-UPON-AVON

Architect: Hathaway family (assumed)
Construction started: 1463
Construction completed: c.1610–1617
Construction materials: Timber frame, limestone, brick, stucco and thatch
Area: Cottage and gardens 0.5sq km (0.2sq miles)
Location: Shottery, Stratford-upon-Avon, United Kingdom

The childhood farmhouse home of William Shakespeare's wife Anne Hathaway illustrates the vernacular Tudor houses and buildings built for ordinary people. These were slow to adopt the latest contemporary trends. They typically had a timber frame filled with wattle and daub; brickwork was sometimes used initially.

Anne Hathaway's Cottage was constructed in two phases. The eastern lower section was originally erected in the mid-15th century and consisted of only three rooms. It was built using the cruck frame method, where the building structure is formed by a pair of long, naturally curved timber members leaning into each other to provide both vertical wall surfaces and the roof supports. The timber frame was set on a limestone plinth and the front door set asymmetrically and approached via two flights of limestone steps. The upper western section and additional sections on the eastern end of the building were built in the 17th century. Multiple tall, red brick chimney stacks rise above the thatched ridge to spread heat evenly around the house during the winter months. The largest of these comes from a fireplace used in the kitchen for cooking. The house has aesthetically pleasing externally visible timber framing and brick and stucco infill. Brickwork was laid using thick joints of lime mortar, allowing for flexibility to accommodate timber frame movement and to make up for any irregularities in the bricks. The building was roofed in thatch with attic dormer casement windows set into the eaves, providing a perfect example of the vernacular Tudor style.

TUDOR GABLE
The pitched thatch roof and end gable, with decorative half-timbering and patterned brickwork infill, houses a typical Tudor-style casement window with diagonal leaded glass panes, set centrally in the gable.

MANUELINE 1490–1550

- Carved **stone** ornamentation with maritime themes and newly discovered lands
- **Columns** carved like **twisted ropes**
- **Bevelled crenellations** at roof level
- Very **ornate portals**

SANTA CRUZ MONASTERY, COIMBRA

Architects: Diogo de Boitaca and Marcos Pires
Construction started: 1132
Construction completed: c.1530, with later additions
Construction materials: Ança limestone
Area: Approx. 954sq m (10,268sq ft)
Location: Coimbra, Portugal

Little remains of the original Romanesque structure at Santa Cruz Monastery, which is thought to have originally had one nave and a high tower. Changes were made to the original building to create the final resting place of the first two kings of Portugal in 1507. The new church and chapter house were constructed with basket-handled rib-vaulted ceilings as well as a new monumental façade with ornate sculptural carvings. The main portal and façade hold symbolically carved ornamentation representing a mixed collection of elements from newly discovered lands and monastic references, to provide new artistic elements such as botanical motifs, navigational instruments and elements found on ships of Manueline and Renaissance inspiration.

The interior space is covered with impressive rib vaults and decorated with Baroque tiles. The ornate niches that form the highly decorative and intricately carved tombs of the kings are placed in front of and at right angles to the main altar behind the main arch framing the altar. The altar appears to be framed by marble columns; however, these are actually wood painted to look like marble. Blue and white Portuguese *azulejos* tiles line the walls of the church and depict key events in Portugal's history. Although these tiles are inconsistent in quality they provide an unusual and beautiful solution to help with acoustics in the church and to cover faded and damaged fresco work from previous applications. The organ is decorated in ornate Japanese artwork and has 4000 pipes, making it extremely challenging to play. Santa Cruz Monastery is one of the most impressive examples of the melding of cultures and historic references that form the Manueline style.

SILENCE CLOISTER
Ribbed vaults and *bas-relief* stone carvings form the ceilings of the cloister, while blue, yellow and white *azulejos* tiles line the base of the walls of the Silence Cloister.

TOMB OF KING SANCHO I (ABOVE)
The Tomb of King Sancho I is one of two tombs, placed on each side of the main altar, holding the remains of the first two kings of Portugal. The tombs are mirror images of each other; they face the head of the church and are surrounded by statues symbolizing bravery, leadership and nobility.

NAVE AND ALTAR (LEFT)
The main altar at the head of the church holds a niche as its focal point furnished with a pyramid of tiers representing stairs to heaven. The walls of the nave are lined with *azulejos* tiles.

HIGH RENAISSANCE 1500–1525

- Pinnacle of Classical **simplicity** and **harmony**
- **Rotational** symmetry, in which the plan can be rotated around its central point
- Simplified Classical orders are perfectly **balanced**

THE TEMPIETTO, ROME

Architect: Donato Bramante
Construction started: 1502
Construction completed: Undocumented
Construction materials: Concrete and marble
Height: 14m (46ft)
Location: Rome, Italy

The Tempietto is a Doric shrine erected upon the traditional site of St Peter's martyrdom. It sits within a quadrilateral courtyard and is only fully visible from one fixed vantage point. The building has a solidity and mass not seen in early Renaissance style and does not strictly adhere to Classical language and order, instead adapting these elements to create a new style. This can be seen in its columns, which are not fluted, giving them a more powerful and purposeful aesthetic. The Tempietto is a single chamber temple comprising a double cylinder arrangement. A circle of Doric columns forms the peristyle (the outer ring of columns) built from both re-used grey granite and new, lighter marble. Windows set within these niches allow daylight in.

The Tempietto's hemispherical dome is supported on a drum of equal height and its interior face is painted with gold stars and a blue background, creating the illusion of a night sky between the dome's structural ribs. Beyond the colonnade to the rear of the temple is a bank of stairs leading down to a sacred crypt. A circular window set into the crypt's ceiling lets one see into this space through the floor. There is little functional purpose to this small temple, but it is seen more as a piece of sculpture than as a usable building. Its plan is rotated around a central point resulting in a circular layout and it has its Classical orders stripped of ornamentation, resulting in balanced simplicity and harmony. The Tempietto is a perfectly proportioned, beautifully sculptured little structure set in a tranquil place with a powerful and uplifting aesthetic that sums up High Renaissance architecture at its best.

ST PETER STATUE
A large niche opposite the entrance holds a statue of St Peter with the keys to the heavenly kingdom in one hand and the gospel in the other. The pedestal below shows a relief carving of his upside-down crucifixion.

MANNERISM 1525–1600

- **Exaggerated** forms
- Surprising **effects** and visual **trickery**
- **Humour** and strange combinations of form, characters, plants, animals and objects
- Rich and **lavish decoration** covering entire surfaces

PALAZZO TE, MANTUA

Architect: Giulio Romano
Construction started: 1524
Construction completed: 1534
Construction materials: Masonry, cut stone and *spezzato*, or broken and blemished plaster
Area: 34,000sq m (365,980sq ft)
Location: Mantua, Lombardy, Italy

Palazzo Te is an excellent example of how palace and villa architecture merged to form a new suburban architecture. It uses a formal square plan with a large cloistered inner courtyard garden and colonnaded outbuildings, and referred to country villas of earlier times, where the building's setting within the landscape was harmonious. It sits low and is horizontally formed, the predominant rooms laid out across the ground floor. The exterior design bears direct resemblance to Classical order and style; however, the four façades are different and the Classical proportioning and references disguise a more playful freedom within the design, probably due to complications arising during the build. The architect cleverly played with the rules of Classical architecture by adding elements of surprise. There are smooth ashlar finishes on some surfaces and rough rustic work surrounding others. Flat pilasters sit against rusticated walls, the façades are not as symmetrical as one may first assume, the spans between the columns are irregular, and the colonnaded walls are decorated by deep niches and blind windows. Intervening surfaces are splattered with *spezzato*, broken and blemished plaster, giving depth and shadow to the surfaces.

The interior ornament and plasterwork took 10 years to carve and paint with frescoes, until there was barely a surface in any part of the building left undecorated. These frescoes are the most remarkable feature of the palazzo and incorporate fantastic scenes, stylized horses, giants and grotesque figures that distort space, making the rooms seem much larger, and therefore more magnificent, than they are in reality.

DAVID'S LOGGIA
This hallway, connecting the interior, courtyard and garden, has columns, sculptures, *bas relief* work and colourful frescoes illustrating King David's heroic deeds and crimes.

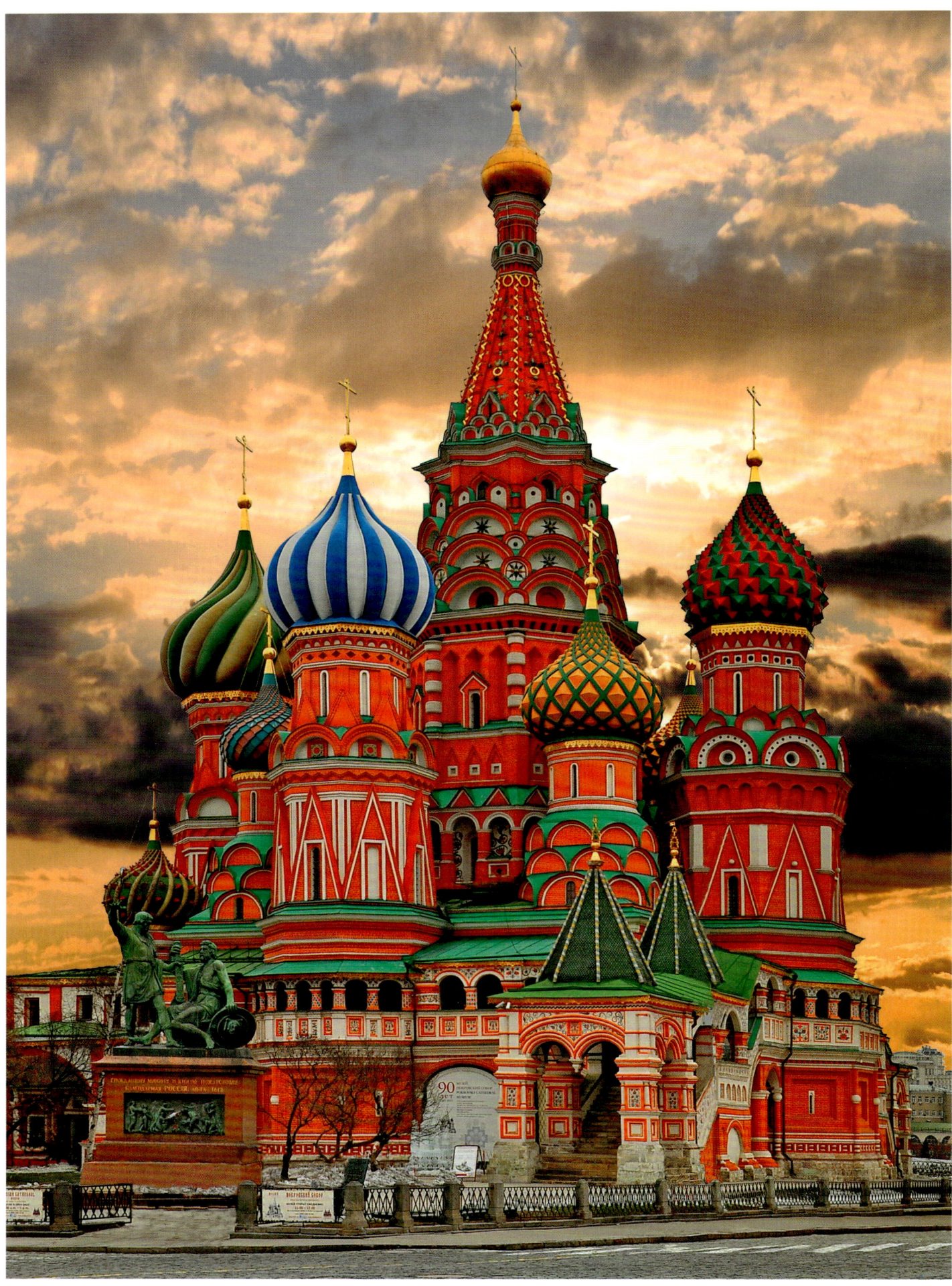

MIDDLE MUSCOVITE 1530–1630

- **High** tented roofs
- Golden **onion domes**
- **White** stone foundations
- Decorative **ornamental masonry** construction

SAINT BASIL'S CATHEDRAL, MOSCOW

Architect: Postnik Yakovlev
Construction started: 1555
Construction completed: 1561
Construction materials: Timber frame encased in brickwork, stone, stucco, wood and tin
Height: 65m (213ft)
Location: Moscow, Russia

Saint Basil's Cathedral in Moscow's Red Square has witnessed many historical and political events. Ivan the Terrible ordered its construction and it is thought the design was meant to resemble flames rising into the sky. This architectural resolution was something that had never been seen before, even in the traditions of Byzantine architecture, and its complexity quickly became the tradition for Russian architecture.

White foundation stones were laid and the church was built in red brick. The basement levels of the building were constructed to accurate measurements, yet the structure becomes less perfectly aligned as it rises from the ground. This has been attributed to the use of an internal timber frame that runs the entire height of the church. This frame was made of tied timber studs and then encased in brickwork afterwards. The movement within the timber frame during the construction would have resulted in the discrepancies as the height of the building increased. The cathedral celebrates complex shapes and architectural ornamentation in brickwork. Brickwork was used purely as decoration both externally and internally, including on the tented roof structure in a highly decorative manner with white stucco added to create contrasting smooth panels. Sculptures, plant motifs and sacred symbols of earlier architecture are not used here and the floral depictions found internally were only added later. The onion domes were covered in tin and gilded, resulting in a church that was highly original, yet with traditional colouring of red brick, white stucco and gold domes. Only later was Saint Basil's Cathedral painted in the bright colours seen today.

ONION DOME
Onion domes are symbolically and technically important. Their height exceeds their width and they taper smoothly to a point. In this way they are able to both portray the tongues of flames, recalling the Holy Spirit, and cope with heavy snowfall.

FLORAL PAINTINGS (ABOVE)
The interior is a maze of galleries winding from chapel to chapel and from one level to another via narrow stairways and low arches. The first floral ornamental murals were added inside these galleries after 1737.

FIGURATIVE MURALS (RIGHT)
In 1737, the cathedral was damaged by fire; during the repairs the first figurative murals were painted inside the building.

MAIN DOME (LEFT)
The largest central main dome of Saint Basil's Cathedral is 46m (151ft) tall internally with a relatively small floor area (64sq m or 690sq ft). Its exceptionally thick brick walls are ornately laid to provide relief patterning and interest to the interior.

ELIZABETHAN 1558–1603

- More **symmetrical** with huge windows
- Renaissance influence in **Classical details**
- **Tall**, decorative chimneys and busy rooflines
- Elaborate **interior** decoration

BURGHLEY HOUSE, STAMFORD

Architect: William Cecil, First Lord Burghley
Construction started: 1555
Construction completed: 1587
Construction materials: Ashlar (finely dressed) Kingscliffe limestone
Area: Approx. 6200sq m (67,000sq ft)
Location: Stamford, United Kingdom

Burghley House, one of the largest and grandest houses built in the Elizabethan age, was designed, built and owned by William Cecil, Elizabeth I's Lord High Treasurer. This spectacular three-storey building constructed with Kingscliffe limestone around a rectangular courtyard is a leading example of the Elizabethan 'prodigy house'. The courtyard is visually anchored by four square corner towers with octagonal turrets and ogee cupolas on top, directly inspired by continental European architectural styles. The magnificent west façade comprises nine bays and features a central gatehouse that projects from the main façade in a bay with four octagonal turrets and cupolas on each side of spectacular golden gates. This was originally intended as the main entrance but that was later moved to the north façade, where it addresses a semi-circular forecourt and driveway later modelled by famed landscape designer Capability Brown.

The main part of the house has 35 major rooms on the ground and first floors and more than 80 lesser rooms. The ground floor interiors are of great internal height; the second floor windows are blank frames because these rooms occupy the full volume of the two floors. These stately rooms have strong European influences and are ornately decorated with carvings modelled on Renaissance and Baroque styles. A magnificent collection of furniture and sumptuous decoration (including original paintings by Old Masters) sit alongside paintings of Roman mythology and ornately executed frescoes. The grand scale of the house and its awe-inspiring architecture, alongside its mixed continental influences and splendid interiors, make it a truly extravagant and perfect example of Elizabethan style.

GOLDEN GATES
These beautiful gates were designed in the late 17th century by Jean Tijou, a Huguenot ironworker, in wrought iron with copper leaf decoration, and gilded by René Cousin.

KEY ARCHITECTURAL STYLES OF THE 17TH CENTURY

BAROQUE (1600–1750)
The Italian Renaissance work of Michelangelo, Palladio and Romano inspired the Baroque style. Wildly exaggerated detailing, deep colours, complex contrasts, grandeur and a sense of surprise all came together to create utterly awe-inspiring architecture. To Baroque architects, a building was a large sculpture. Therefore with each structure they created their own interpretation of Baroque characteristics, to develop their own regional Baroque architecture.

JACOBEAN (1603–25)
During the reign of King James I of England, architects developed new ideas that combined elements of previous architectural styles and novel European ideas to form his namesake Jacobean style. This displayed opulence and saw a development of the 'prodigy house' from the Elizabethan era. Materials like brick and stone were used, with limestone and slate detailing on façades and ornate decoration internally in granite and fine woodwork.

PALLADIAN (1615–90)
Palladian architecture was strongly influenced by the Italian 16th-century architect Andrea Palladio. After studying Palladio's work and visiting his architecture in Italy, the English architect Inigo Jones brought his vision to England and set about designing a new architecture based on Palladio's ideas. Exteriors were characterized by their Classical forms, strict proportion, symmetry and somewhat austere façades. However, the interiors were more elaborate and decorative, with gilding and fresco paintings used to create grand and opulent spaces.

LATE MUSCOVITE (1630–1712)
During this period, the Russian state was not as wealthy as previously, and rich merchants gave financial backing for various construction projects. They built much smaller church structures than before, still with onion domes and tented roofs, but moving away from asymmetrical to symmetrical plans. Brick exteriors became more elaborate and towards the end of the 17th century tented roof structures were banned, replaced with the successive rows of corbelled brick arches that became Moscow's flamboyant hallmark style.

ROCOCO (EARLY 17TH TO MID-18TH CENTURY)
Rococo has its roots in late Baroque architecture and is French in origin. Its defining characteristic is its decorative style, with exaggerated fluid-form ornamentation and lighter colours, often using pastel shades. Shapes are complex, asymmetrical and more playful. Walls, ceilings and mouldings have interlacing curves and naturalistic forms, elaborate scrolls and intricate and delicately carved details. Gilding was intentionally spare, and mirrors were used frequently to create the illusion of more space.

MUGHAL (1550–1760)
Mughal style, which developed in northern and central India under the Mughal emperors, referenced the symmetry and decorative styles of Indian, Turkish and Persian architecture and signified a revival of Islamic architecture. It originated with the use of red sandstone and later employed white marble, blending various provincial styles to produce remarkably refined structures. Symmetry and balance are paramount and the delicacy of detail in the decorative work has seldom been surpassed.

17TH-CENTURY ARCHITECTURE

A culmination of learning and the redistribution of power, which was increasingly centralized in bureaucratic princely states, saw 17th-century Europe enter a period known as the General Crisis, resulting in the English Civil War and other revolts. The European architecture of the period saw a return to Classical rules, with far greater exuberance.

Henry IV, Louis XIII and Louis XIV boldly imposed absolute monarchy in France by depleting the power of the nobility. However, this came at great expense: there were 232 popular uprisings in France between 1635 and 1660. In England, the 17th century was no less eventful. Charles I ascended to the throne in 1625, but by 1649 he had been executed and the Commonwealth was established in place of the monarchy. The Great Fire of London in 1666 decimated the capital, which took years to rebuild. The French took full advantage of this period of weakness, declaring war on England that same year. Russia experienced its own 'Time of Troubles', only achieving stability under the Western-influenced rule of Peter the Great from the 1680s. In India, the Mughal empire, at its peak in the 17th century, spanned 4,000,000sq km (1,500,000sq miles), becoming an economic and manufacturing superpower in what is considered the country's last golden age. The 17th century was also a revolutionary time, when maths, science and reason came to the fore, putting mysticism and superstition on the back foot. Great thinkers such as Galileo, Blaise Pascal and Isaac Newton established scientific principles that would later make the Industrial Revolution possible.

INTRICATE DECORATION ON THE TAJ MAHAL
Inside the 1643 mosque just to the west of the Taj Mahal mausoleum, the grand archways are decorated with stucco inlaid stonework.

BAROQUE 1600–1750

- **Façades** viewed as architectural 'sculpture'
- **Colossal** order where Classical columns reach two or more storeys
- **Windows** now **rectangular** with rounded tops, rather than Classical

PALACE OF VERSAILLES

Architects: Louis Le Vau, Jules Hardouin-Mansart and others
Construction started: 1623 (hunting lodge)
Construction completed: 1710 (with completion of the chapel)
Construction materials: Brick, white ashlar stone and marble
Area: 63,154sq m (679,784sq ft)
Location: Versailles, France

This huge palace complex started life as a two-storey hunting lodge for Louis XIII in red brick and stone on the site of the current palace's black and white marble courtyard. Some of the original building remains and is part of the central core, but was transformed by Louis XIV. The first phase saw the addition of two wings to the forecourt; one for servants and kitchens and the other for stables. Three new, almost flat-roofed wings were then added and clad in cut white ashlar stone. The exterior was constructed with decorative sculptural features consisting of columns and arcades, a rusticated ground floor, and a first floor with round-headed windows divided by relief arch sculptures and pilasters, some opening onto balconies. The attic floor is demarcated by square windows and pilaster detailing. Colossal pilasters were used on corners to visually tie the façades together. This was topped with a flat roof disguised by balustrading and more ornate sculptured trophies and flame pots. The first floor facing the garden had two symmetrical sets of apartments, one for the king and one for the queen. These were separated by a marble terrace with a central fountain, later removed to create the Hall of Mirrors.

Interior decoration of the palace consists of elaborate sculptures, paintings and ornately crafted frescoes. The Hall of Mirrors was built to provide opulence on the grandest scale. Marble pilasters, detailed gilded relief work, intricately painted frescoes and daylight are reflected around the room by the row of 17 mirror-clad arches, each with 21 mirrors, to form true Baroque extravagance.

FRESCOES IN THE ROYAL CHAPEL
The Royal Chapel, as seen from the Royal Gallery, has two levels. The king and family worshipped in the upper Royal Gallery, while others used the ground floor. The ceiling is painted with beautiful fresco scenes.

GARDENS (ABOVE)
The vast gardens of Versailles cover around 8sq km (3sq miles), most of which is landscaped in the classic 'French garden' style with fountains, canals and geometrically formal planting designed by André le Nôtre.

HALL OF MIRRORS (LEFT)
The Hall of Mirrors and central gallery is a remarkable construction. Seventeen mirror-clad arches reflect the 17 arcaded windows that look out over the gardens, while each arch has 21 mirrors, totalling 357 mirrors decorating the room. The arches are fixed between marble pilasters with gilded bronze capitals of *fleur-de-lys* and Gallic cockerels.

JACOBEAN 1603–25

- Large **symmetrical Flemish gables** on front façades
- **Flat** roofs with window bays
- **Stone** mullioned windows
- Highly **ornamented interiors**

HATFIELD HOUSE

Architects: Robert Lyminge, Simon Basil and Inigo Jones
Construction started: 1608
Construction completed: 1612
Construction materials: Brick and stone
Area: Approx. 6395sq m (68,835sq ft)
Location: Hertfordshire, United Kingdom

Hatfield House, a large country house set in extensive parkland, is one of the most important Jacobean mansions in England and is typical of the period and style. The house consists of a central main area with symmetrical wings either side to form a U-shaped plan, with the main ground-floor rooms used as public social areas and the upper floors as private quarters. The house displays the relatively simple façades of Jacobean architecture, yet on closer inspection has plenty of detailing. Red brick was reused from the demolished royal palace previously built on the site to form the new stone-dressed red-brick house.

Within the U-shaped courtyard, the central building's inner façade is dressed stone, creating a beautiful aesthetic different from the surrounding red brickwork. A series of open arches delineated by pilasters reminiscent of Palladian Classical orders form a loggia along the ground floor, behind which sits the exquisite Long Gallery. The loggia supports the upper façade set out in rigid symmetry with stone mullion windows topped with stone balustrading at roofline. Flemish gables set back from the façade provide detail to the flat roof. The two wings are decorated with lead cupola domed corner tower projections; they differ from the central volume in that they are less elaborate, in red brick and with pitched roofs.

The statement staircase is the focal point of the house's interior and features elaborate wooden lions and cupids carved into the balusters and newel posts. Flemish- and French-inspired ornamental carvings cover the interior walls, fireplaces, window frames and ceilings. Hatfield House exemplifies Jacobean style, with its relatively simple yet refined exterior and interior opulence designed to impress while entertaining.

ELABORATE CEILING
The 52-m (170ft) Long Gallery carved plaster ceiling has remained unchanged since it was built, except for its later gilding. It consists of a heavily symbolic pattern of bands enclosing heraldic panels.

PALLADIAN 1615–90

- **Classical** forms, strict proportion and symmetry
- **Austere**, plain façades
- Central **arched** windows with flanking rectangular sections
- Interior **ornamentation gilding** and frescoes creating opulent spaces

QUEEN'S HOUSE, GREENWICH

Architect: Inigo Jones
Construction started: 1616
Construction completed: 1635
Construction materials: Masonry of brick and stone, render
Area: Approx. 5,500sq m (59,200sq ft)
Location: Greenwich, London, United Kingdom

Queen's House was built for Anne of Denmark, wife of King James I, and was a remarkable deviation from the previous tradition of red-brick Tudor-style buildings. It is a true example of Palladian architectural influence, with its elegant proportions, well-balanced façade, rusticated ground floor, central loggia with plain wings, and high-quality interiors.

Queen's House was built over a road connecting the royal shipyards; to accommodate this, the ground floor originally consisted of two rectangular blocks connected at first floor by a bridge. This H-shaped plan was later adapted and two further bridges were added either side of the original bridge, filling the voids to form a square. One building holds the Great Hall, a two-storey cube with upper cantilevered gallery and a black and white patterned marble floor, its geometry mirrored in the ornate decoration of the ceiling. The opposite building holds the Ionic loggia overlooking Greenwick Park. The bridge is accessed via the beautiful tulip spiral staircase, the first of its kind in England. Either side of this central axis comprising the hall, bridge and loggia are two suites of rooms, providing a symmetrical plan of equal proportions.

The building's façades are typically Palladian, consisting of three elements with a central projecting portion. The walls are rusticated at ground floor level, plain on the upper level and topped with a flat roof surrounded by a masonry parapet balustrade. Classical order columns and pilasters are not seen on the main façades of the house but only in the Ionic loggia; instead, Inigo Jones used Classical proportion, rustication and balustrading to provide a simplified silhouette for this style of architecture.

TULIP STAIRS
This delicately ornate staircase sweeps up through the building, sheathed in daylight and framed by a wrought iron flower balustrade spiralling up the outer edge. It was the first centrally unsupported spiral staircase in England.

THE COLONNADES (ABOVE)
In 1807, two symmetrical Ionic colonnades were added to join Queen's House to two new accommodation wings, after it was decided that the building would be used as the Royal Hospital School.

THE GREAT HALL (RIGHT)
The Great Hall is the centrepiece of Queen's House. It was conceived as a perfect cube with an encircling cantilevered gallery set halfway up its height. The striking black and white marble floor and ceiling patterning echo each other.

THE KING'S PRESENCE CHAMBER (LEFT)
Visitors pass from the upper gallery of the Great Hall into the King's Presence Chambers. These have bright blue colour on the walls and gold highlights on the elaborately carved ceilings and wall panels.

LATE MUSCOVITE 1630–1712

- Churches **smaller** in size
- Highly decorated **onion domes**, tented structures and, later on, corbelled brick arches
- **Highly decorated** red brick exteriors
- Profuse **decoration** internally

CHURCH OF THE INTERCESSION AT FILI, MOSCOW

Architect: Unknown, built for Lev Naryshkin
Construction started: 1689
Construction completed: 1694
Construction materials: Brick and timber
Area: Approx. 2200sq m (23,700sq ft)
Location: Moscow, Russia

The Church of the Intercession at Fili is one of the most beautiful churches in Moscow. It actually consists of two churches within one: a winter intercession church in the basement and a summer (unheated) church dedicated to the Saviour above it. The church is built on a traditional Greek cross layout with four rounded ends, each terminating in a pointed cupola. This forms an unusual *quatrefoil* shape (or ornamental design of four lobes) with three ornate external staircases. Unusually, the church belfry is internalized, with the bells hanging inside the upper reaches of the church. The church has five domes with one set centrally.

Inside the church, arches were predominantly used for decorative purposes. During renovation work, original paintwork of frescoes dating back around 200 years was revealed in the central vault under the main dome of the tallest tower. The exterior is enchanting in its elegance and the delicate white stone lace carvings set against the red brickwork of the main structure, topped off with glowing golden onion domes, makes the building seem light, intricate and almost mystical. The interior decoration and ornamentation mimics the ornately elaborate delicacy found on the exterior of the church. The upper church is decorated in a gilded tiered iconostasis (a wall of icons and religious ornamentation) that reaches all the way up to the underside of the main dome. This iconostasis is intricately decorated, with beautifully carved and gilded floral ornamentation making the altar appear as though it is reaching for the heavens.

GILDED ICONOSTASIS
The oldest oak altar in Russia is decorated with a gilded and tiered iconostasis that reaches up to the ceiling of the main central dome, where traces have been found of 200-year-old vault frescoes.

ROCOCO EARLY 17TH TO MID-18TH CENTURY

- **Ornate** style with soft angles and curves
- **Lightness** in colour and weight
- **Low relief** work of ribbons, scrolls, shells, flower wreaths, birds and animals

SCHÖNBRUNN PALACE

Architects: Joseph Emanuel Fischer von Erlach, Nikolaus Pacassi and Johann Aman
Construction Started: 1696
Construction Completed: 1819
Construction Materials: Masonry
Area: Approx. 8000m sq (86,000 sq ft)
Location: Vienna, Austria

This property originated in the 14th century, with the first substantial country estate seen in 1548. In 1569, the Habsburg monarchy took possession and in 1642 Eleonora von Gonzaga renamed it Schönbrunn and built a *château de plaisance*. Turkish troops plundered it in the siege of Vienna and in 1686 Italian Baroque architect Fischer von Erlach was commissioned by Emperor Leopold I to design an imperial hunting lodge here for his son and heir Joseph. In 1696 it was built on the existing *château de plaisance* foundations, and by 1700 the central building was completed in line with symmetrical Baroque design principles. Emperor Charles VI acquired the property in 1728 and gave it to his daughter, Maria Theresa. This is the notable period when Schönbrunn became the centre of court and political life. Under her and architect Nikolaus Pacassi it was rebuilt into a palatial summer residence. The palace complex changed extensively over Maria Theresa's reign, but the Rococo detailing for which Schönbrunn is so famous can be attributed to her and her architect. They saw to the adornment of the exterior with detailed articulation and rich ornamentation, resulting in a great example of Rococo architecture. Stucco marble was added to the vaulted ceilings in the Galleries. Frescoed ceilings were painted, and then magnificent stucco decoration added, resulting in some of the most important Rococo interiors ever created. Rooms on the garden side of the palace had typical Rococo decoration of playful exuberant rocaille (a French style of decoration) forms with mirrors and paintings set into the walls. The 1770s saw the last project carried out under Maria Theresa, with work on the gardens and construction of garden features like the Gloriette.

GLORIETTE CEILING
Highly detailed in deep relief, the sculptural plaster decorations on the ceiling of the Gloriette were executed by Benedikt Henrici, with typical reference to ribbons, plant wreaths and scrolls.

MUGHAL 1550–1760

- Massive **vaulted** gateways
- Slender **minarets** with **cupolas** at four corners
- The bulbous **dome**
- Delicate **ornamentation**

TAJ MAHAL, AGRA

Architect: Attributed to Ustad Ahmad Lahauri
Construction started: 1632
Construction completed: 1653
Construction materials: White marble
Height: 73m (240ft)
Location: Agra, India

The Taj Mahal is an architectural masterpiece built by Mughal emperor Shah Jahan as a mausoleum for his wife Mumtaz Mahal, and both rest in this white marble monument to love. More than 20,000 craftsmen worked on the building, which consists of white marble and 28 types of precious and semi-precious stones from around India and Asia. Four tall minarets frame the tomb, each divided into three parts by two balconies, and a final balcony at the top is roofed with a *chhatri* (an ornate dome-like pavilion structure). The tomb addresses the main approach, with an arched doorway enclosed within a *pishtaq* or rectangular black marble calligraphic framework set into white marble. Two more arched balconies on each side make the design symmetrical. The domes and vaults are worked with tracery and incised painting, creating elaborate geometric forms. The tomb's lower walls hold white marble dado sculptures in *bas-relief* showing flowers and vines. Doorways and arches are decorated with *pietra dura* inlays of vines, flowers and fruit.

The main chamber holds the sarcophagi, while the actual burial sites are underground. Detailed and delicately cut precious and semi-precious gems are inlaid into the white marble of the tomb and cenotaphs. The tomb is roofed with a spectacular large marble onion dome, while tall thin decorative spires extending from the edges of the roof provide further vertical emphasis. The dome, four surrounding *chhatris* and four minaret *chhatris* are topped by domes with a lotus design and gilded finials that bring light into inner areas. Together, the exterior and interior of the Taj Mahal make it an awe-inspiring achievement of Mughal architecture and like nothing else built since.

CHHATRIS
Chhatris located on the main building, as well as on the minarets around the Taj Mahal, share the same decorative lotus design topped by a gilded finial.

CENOTAPHS WITH *PIETRA DURA* (ABOVE)
The tomb in the inner Taj Mahal holds two cenotaphs, one for Shah Jahan and one for his wife Mumtaz Mahal. Both are elegantly carved and inlaid in *pietra dura* (marble inlay work) made with thousands of precious and semi-precious gemstones.

ISLAMIC MOTIFS (RIGHT)
Simple forms of carved and interlaced geometric, calligraphic or plant-like motifs are used to adorn Islamic and Mughal architecture.

INCISED PAINTING (LEFT)
Archways are decorated with incised painting, a technique used to decorate stone surfaces. A channel is scratched into the stone surface and then covered with a thick layer of paint or stucco; when dry it is scraped off, leaving the painted decoration in the surface.

KEY ARCHITECTURAL STYLES OF THE 18TH CENTURY

PETRINE BAROQUE (1690–1730)
Russian architecture during this period became influenced by the Baroque style from further afield. As this spread through Russia, the traditional architecture of the past was replaced with a more refined Baroque style of simple volumes, flat façades and a high level of interior decoration, as favoured by Peter the Great.

AMERICAN COLONIAL (1600–1900)
As England established its first colonies in North America, early colonial architecture followed the English Jacobean and Georgian style, although Dutch, French and Spanish influences also appeared. Distance and adaptability to local conditions led to this simpler style in North America.

QUEEN ANNE (1702–14)
This style developed in Great Britain during Queen Anne's reign. Palatial red brick manor houses with large flush sash windows were built, pouring daylight into their impressive interior spaces. These structures were usually two rooms deep with Classical proportions and symmetrical façades.

GEORGIAN (1714–1830)
Georgian architecture became a model for architectural style elsewhere in the world, including the colonies. Buildings were characterized by symmetry and a replication of the Classical proportions of Roman architecture, and usually made of local brick and stone.

NEOCLASSICAL (1750–1900)
In the second half of the 18th century, as European kingdoms, American colonial states and Russian cities grew, they looked to the past traditions in architecture for legitimacy and started to use the Classical architectural forms and styles in a new way, resulting in Neoclassical architecture. Simple flat façades were used with expressed simplified columns and Classical order.

GOTHIC REVIVAL (1760–1930)
The Gothic Revival style drew upon a romanticized view of medieval history and architecture. The style was used prolifically in Great Britain and the United States. This revival drew on traditional Gothic features such as finials, castle-like towers and decorative façades; however, every element was exaggerated vertically.

POMBALINE (1755–1800)
Pombaline style was named after the first Marquis of Pombal, who redesigned Lisbon after the 1755 earthquake. Pombaline has its roots in medieval, Renaissance and Baroque architecture. However, its works arose as a necessity rather than an ornament and were more modest than previous styles.

FEDERAL (1780–1830)
Federal architecture saw the end of the Colonial era and represented a new beginning. Americans wanted their architecture to express new ideals of democracy and to convey prosperity. As a result, it progressed from the Georgian influences of American Colonial style with the addition of more elaborate decorations.

JEFFERSONIAN (1790–1830)
Thomas Jefferson advocated the use of formal rules of Palladianism and ancient Roman architecture, resulting in the Jeffersonian style. Government buildings were even modelled on entire Roman temples.

18TH-CENTURY ARCHITECTURE

Huge advances in philosophy and science during the Enlightenment culminated in the American and French revolutions. But monarchies across Europe, at first keen to support this new era of growth, reacted and retrenched when they witnessed the Reign of Terror in France of 1793–1794.

In Russia, Peter the Great took the momentous decision to 'Westernize' his country, while simultaneously retaining strong elements of indigenous culture. This was a time of great economic growth for Russia and large new cities sprang up, including Yekaterinodar, Yekaterinburg, Yekaterinoslav, Saint Petersburg and Sevastopol. At the same time, Russia expanded territorially, both west and eastwards. In post-revolution America, a new system of federal governance was being tried and tested. Meanwhile, an evangelical revival known as the Great Awakening swept across the newly independent continent, acting as a tool to galvanize the separate states as one community. The 18th century saw the industrial revolution change Great Britain unrecognizably. The introduction of steam power and mass production in machinery-driven factories caused cities to grow exponentially as the masses migrated to find work.

In eastern Europe, this century saw the end of the once powerful Polish-Lithuanian Commonwealth. Multiple invasions by the Austrian and Russian empires, and the kingdom of Prussia, eroded the once vast state. The three attackers divided the territories among themselves, and the ramifications of this action lasted for the next 100 years.

VILNIUS CATHEDRAL PORTICO
The tympanum, or decorative triangle over the entrance, illustrates in *bas-relief* a carving of the story of Noah.

PETRINE BAROQUE 1690–1730

- A main **central building** with **two wings**
- **Simple** forms and **flat** façades
- **High** level of interior decoration
- **Noble** materials used internally

GRAND MENSHIKOV PALACE, ORANIENBAUM

Architects: Giovanni Maria Fontana, Gottfried Schädel, Francesco Bartolomeo Rastrelli and Antonio Rinaldi
Construction started: 1710
Construction completed: 1762
Construction materials: Stone
Area: Approx. 7000sq m (75,000sq ft)
Location: Lomonosov, near Saint Petersburg, Russia

The Grand Palace combines western European Baroque with elements of traditional Russian architecture, resulting in Petrine Baroque. Architects of Italian origin and western European craftsmen were involved in building the palace, bringing a wealth of European influence. Built by Prince Menshikov, Peter the Great's closest adviser, the palace was the largest and most spectacular in the region. Its hillside location on the Gulf of Finland adds to its immensity, giving the impression that it hovers over the shoreline. The palace's magnificence, simple curvaceous presence and sumptuous interiors made it a marvel.

The main façade sits on a two-tier terrace. The palace's centrepiece is a two-storey central block with a princely crown at roof level, while two concave single-storey galleried side wings project in sweeping curves that terminate with two octagonal domed pavilions, the Palace Chapel and the Japanese Pavilion (named after its porcelain collection). These pavilions complete the rear garden courtyard by extending into two additional single-storey wings running at right angles to the main building. The complex is a perfect example of Petrine Baroque, with its characteristic symmetry, simplicity of dimension and volume, and flat façades broken up rhythmically by modestly ornamented pillars and varying colour tones. Interiors were decorated with noble materials to a high level of detail, at huge expense. The Eastern Gallery featured a Turkish bath and paintings on canvas, tapestries, marble, decorative Delft tiles from the Netherlands, relief wooden wall panelling, and patterned timber parquet flooring.

PALACE CHAPEL
The octagonal Palace Chapel pavilion sits at the end of the curved single storey gallery and is set on a two-tiered terrace facing the sea.

AMERICAN COLONIAL 1600–1900

- Highly **symmetrical**
- Roofs are **gabled**, gambrel or hipped
- **Portico** at the main entrance
- **Dormer** windows at upper floors or roof
- **Larger** rectangular multipaned windows

OLD STATE HOUSE, BOSTON

Architect: Unknown
Construction started: 1712
Construction completed: 1713
Construction materials: Brick
Height: 11.35m (37ft)
Location: Boston, Massachusetts, USA

The Old State House is the oldest surviving public building in Boston; it is not only important architecturally, but also historically and politically. American Colonial buildings took on many influences from colonizing countries, and the Old State House's roots lie in English Georgian architecture. The red brick two-and-a-half-storey structure is highly symmetrical. Its gambrel (two-sided, double-sloped) roof is obscured by gable ends and there are pedimented dormer sash windows in its slopes. The original gilded lion and aluminium leaf unicorn, symbols of British royal authority, are prominently positioned on each side of the gables, having been removed after independence and later reinstated. A tiered tower rises mid-roof, with large arched windows, ornate tracery, Doric corner pilasters and a Classical frieze. The Old State House's balcony is framed by fluted Corinthian pilasters supporting a Classical pediment.

The recessed central entrances have elaborate American colonial doorways with fluted Doric columns and pediments, and the door jambs were rusticated to imitate dressed ashlar stone. The timber sash windows are multipaned, with embellished splayed brick lintels. This formal ornamentation and strict symmetry are reminiscent of Classical styles and reference high Georgian design. Internally, buildings in this style show a distinct interpretation of Georgian decoration throughout. Internal circulation is via a central spiral staircase connecting the floors and rising through a central rotunda. Georgian details include wide floorboards, doors with moulded architraves, entablatures and cornicing, and a Doric cornice with fret dentil trim. As a whole, the Old State House represents American Colonial style at its best.

SPIRAL STAIRCASE
The open string spiral staircase sweeps through the central rotunda. It features alternating barley and 'Solomonic twist' (spiralling shaft) balusters, as well as tread ends adorned with applied scrollwork.

QUEEN ANNE 1702–14

- **Formal** elevations
- Roofs were often hipped with **dormers**
- **Decorative** embellishment with tile motifs
- Classical **theme** without following **all** the rules of proportion

BLUECOAT CHAMBERS, LIVERPOOL

Architects: Edward Litherland and Thomas Steers
Construction started: 1716
Construction completed: 1717
Construction materials: Brick and stone
Area: Approx. 3654 sq m (39,330 sq ft)
Location: Liverpool, United Kingdom

Bluecoat Chambers is the oldest building in the centre of Liverpool. It was constructed as a charity school, then extended to become a boarding school. Later it underwent further reworkings and had several different uses, including as a school of architecture. Currently it operates as an arts centre. With its brick façades and detailed stone dressings, it is a fine example of a later version of Queen Anne architecture.

The structure consists of a core building with two side wings to make an H-shaped building around a courtyard. The core is symmetrical and consists of five bays, three storeys in height, with a basement. The three central bays project under a pediment that holds a clock. The main entrance is marked by a round-headed doorway framed in architrave and Ionic columns with a segmented pediment. The windows in the central block have rounded heads with ornate architraves and cherub head details on their keystones, and are set into further architraved round-arched reveals. A stone plinth with rusticated quoins (masonry blocks at the wall corners), flat bands and decorative cornices tie the courtyard façades together visually. Each wing has characteristic 'bull's-eye' windows to the basement and top floor. Other windows along these façades are rectangular sash windows with brick lintels and carved keystones. The building has a central octagonal cupola with round arched openings, attached Ionic columns and a copper cap and finial. The striking façade, Classical columns, arched window ornamentation, bull's-eye windows and cherub keystones of Bluecoat Chambers make it an excellent example of Queen Anne architecture, which influenced a number of other contemporary buildings in Liverpool.

BULL'S-EYE WINDOW
Round 'bull's-eye' windows were typical of Queen Anne style. They are an ornamental window set in a circular frame typically found in an upper storey.

GEORGIAN 1714–1830

- **Classical** features derived from Roman architecture
- Made using **luxurious** and **substantial** materials
- **Façades** highlighted extreme symmetry
- Hipped roofs fringed with **dentil mouldings**

THE CIRCUS, BATH

Architects: John Wood the Elder and John Wood the Younger
Construction started: 1754
Construction completed: 1768
Construction materials: Bath stone
Length: 200m (700ft)
Location: Bath, Somerset, United Kingdom

The Circus was a huge achievement in Georgian urban planning and architectural resolution. It consists of three terraces of houses curving around a circular outdoor space. The original plan included a grand circus for the exhibition of sports and a royal forum and imperial gymnasium, all harking back to imperial Rome. Over time, these grand plans were reduced significantly; however, the circular terraces were realized and became a landmark structure in Bath. Two obvious references served as inspiration for the Circus: the Colosseum in Rome, with its Doric, Ionic and Corinthian columns; and the circular stone formations found at prehistoric sites from ancient Celtic cultures.

Basic geometry played an important part in setting out the buildings. An equilateral triangle can be drawn between the three main entry points, ensuring that when viewed from any entry point the Classical façade is always seen square on, completing its perfect symmetry. Three Classical orders are placed one above the other on the façades, with Doric columns at ground level, Ionic at first floor and Corinthian at the upper level. The placement of these columns on a continuous curve creates a wonderful rhythm across the façades. The frieze between the ground and first floor is a Doric entablature of Classical reference, and is covered in pictorial emblems. The parapet at roof level is decorated with stone carvings of acorns, possibly referring back to the idea of druids and prehistoric stone formations. The open space at the centre of The Circus was paved with stone sets that covered a reservoir for water supply to the houses.

DENTIL CORNICE
Stone dentil cornicing is displayed just below the roof parapet on the upper floor of the classically proportioned façade of the Circus.

CRESCENT-SHAPED FAÇADE
Golden-coloured local Bath stone was used for the elegant Georgian façades. The Circus's three storeys are perfectly proportioned by the vertical arrangement of the Classical orders of Doric, Ionic and Corinthian columns, punctured by window openings, to create an excellent example of Georgian rhythm and order.

NEOCLASSICAL 1750–1900

- Buildings were built to be **ostentatious**
- Dramatic and **ornamental** columns gave the buildings a presence
- **Simplistic** geometric forms enhanced by **tall** parapets
- **Flat** façade

VILNIUS CATHEDRAL

Architect: Laurynas Gucevičius
Construction started: 1779
Construction completed: 1783
Construction materials: Masonry and stucco
Height of belfry: 52m (171ft)
Location: Vilnius, Lithuania

The Cathedral Basilica of Saint Stanislaus and Saint Ladislaus of Vilnius is Lithuania's most important Catholic church. The original church dates back to 1251 and has been rebuilt and altered several times, with some elements being retained where possible, although the current Neoclassical structure is the result of major reconstruction in 1779.

The rectangular cathedral is classically imposing, well proportioned and symmetrical. It has 11 lateral chapels, a sacristy and north and south side entrances, while a monumentally proportioned portico at the western end forms the main church façade and entrance. Symmetrical cupolas are placed at the basilica's eastern end and colonnades line both sides, while its domes have lamps and helmets with crosses. There is also a free-standing belfry, built on the ground floor remains of the original lower castle defence tower found on the site before the current church's construction. The impressive front portico is decorated with six colossal Doric columns. The tympanum, or decorative triangle over the entrance, illustrates in *bas-relief* a carving of the story of Noah. The front pediment is topped by three monumental figures of St Casimir, St Helena and St Stanislaus and the portico ceiling is covered in repetitive friezework and carvings in *bas-relief*. The main façade is adorned with sculptures of the four evangelists set into niches. The wall of the main façade is expressed in simple ways with clean lines and flat, smooth stucco. Drama is created by using ornamental columns on a large portico to give the building presence. The influence of Palladian architecture is clearly visible in the side façades of the main structure; these Classical elements, together with the incorporation of Baroque sculptures and other *bas-relief* elements, make Vilnius Cathedral truly Neoclassical.

BAS-RELIEF WORK
Repetitive *bas-relief* work on the ceilings provides interest and shows Rococo influence in the detailing.

GOTHIC REVIVAL 1760–1930

- **Lace** and **lattice** detailing
- Steep pointed roofs with **front-facing** gables
- Ornate **wooden trim** details, often referred to as 'gingerbread' finishes
- **Picturesque** and **romantic** qualities

CHURCH OF SAINT PETER AND SAINT PAUL, OSTEND

Architect: Louis Delacenserie
Construction started: 1899
Construction completed: 1908
Construction materials: Stone and timber
Height: 72m (236ft)
Location: Ostend, Belgium

The Church of Saint Peter and Saint Paul is a Roman Catholic Neo-Gothic church built on the site of a previous church that was destroyed by fire. The architect was inspired by Cologne's Gothic cathedral and the Neo-Gothic Votive Church in Vienna. The façade has two very slim belfry towers and three gabled portals. The nave has a grand rose window, a stone transept spire and buttress abutments (buttresses pulled in close to the walls). Between the doors at the main entrance stands a statue of the Virgin Mary with baby Jesus; on either side there are statues of the church's patron saints, Peter and Paul. Severely sloping roofs and very tall spires provide an exaggerated verticality, as do the parapet and roof edges, which are decorated with ornate pointed finials to emphasize height; none of these elements were seen previously in Gothic architecture. Windows are taller and narrower, arches are pointed, and the building carries an exaggerated ornateness typical of the Gothic Revival style.

The windows tell the story of Ostend and depict religious and historical figures, including Belgian monarchs along the south transept, while the grand rose window is flanked by blind arches. The beautiful original stained-glass windows were destroyed in the two world wars and later replaced. The Queen's Chapel, in green and white marble, is richly decorated with gargoyles and sculptures of canonized queens. Elsewhere the interiors feature elements in Gothic Revival style including stone statues of the evangelists, a white stone cloister in *bas-relief*, oak choir stalls, stone communion rails, a marble pulpit and a copper font.

GOTHIC REVIVAL FINIALS
The Gothic Revival saw the exaggeration of the finial element to give vertical emphasis to the roofline for decorative purposes.

LARGE WINDOWS (ABOVE)
The tall stone mullioned windows are framed by ribbed vaults supported on clustered columns. These huge windows hold an expanse of intricate stone tracery infilled with stained glass, which beautifully illuminates the interior with daylight.

INTRICATE FAÇADE (LEFT)
One of the church's stone façades displays intricate sculptures and gargoyles, ogival (pointed) arches framing windows and tall, slender, sharply pointed spires in the background.

117

POMBALINE 1755–1800

- **Restrained** Neoclassical style
- **Standardized** decoration due to cost and time implications
- Built around a **grid** plan with **fixed** roads and pavement sizes

PRAÇA DO COMÉRCIO, LISBON

Architects: Eugénio dos Santos and Veríssimo da Costa
Construction started: 1755
Construction completed: 1873
Construction materials: Wood, limestone and other stones in prefabricated pieces
Area: 35,000sq m (376,700sq ft)
Location: Lisbon, Portugal

The Pombaline style introduced new construction methods for dealing with earthquake movement, as well as early prefabricated methods of construction. A flexible wooden structure was used within walls, floors and roofs, then covered with pre-manufactured building parts constructed off site and transported in pieces to the city to be assembled. Where ground was unstable, logs were also buried to build upon. After the Lisbon earthquake of 1755 destroyed nearly the entire city, the Marquis of Pombal took charge of its reconstruction, resulting in an orthogonal city grid plan with a more modern design allowing for large open spaces with better light and ventilation. This plan included a large new square, the Praça do Comércio (Commerce Square). The square looks onto the Tagus River on one side and is bordered on the other three sides by stately government buildings with rhythmic arcades facing onto the square and twin towers addressing the river. A spectacular statue of King José I on horseback was placed centrally in front of the magnificently ornate arch built to symbolize triumph over the earthquake.

The buildings surrounding the square are rectangular structures up to four storeys high with open uniform arcades at ground floor level to allow for shops and public spaces, and yellow-coloured upper storeys occupied by administrative functions. Balconies face the square at first floor and attic level. This style can be seen in all Pombaline buildings, although decorative detailing on the façades varies slightly, depending on each building's importance and its function. This architectural style shows strong Neoclassical characteristics, without the presence of formal Classical elements.

PARAPET BALUSTRADING
Pombaline buildings have low-pitched clay tile roofs and simple rectangular attic windows with parapet balconies.

FEDERAL 1780–1830

- Highly **symmetrical**
- More **ornate** elements than Colonial style
- Rounded or arched windows with **elaborate mouldings**
- **Tall, narrow** buildings

OLD TOWN HALL, SALEM

Architects: Attributed to Charles Bulfinch
Construction started: 1816
Construction completed: 1817
Construction materials: Brick
Area: Approx. 613sq m (6600sq ft)
Address: Salem, Massachusetts, USA

The Old Town Hall is one of the few surviving municipal buildings in Salem and a true example of Federal style. The ground level was designed and used as a public market, while the upper floor housed a public Great Hall and the town offices. Georgian influences continued to be used in Federal-style buildings such as the Old Town Hall, and Classical proportion and symmetry on façades remained prevalent. However, this style moved towards a flatter façade without Classical orders of columns, porticos and heavy ornamentation, resulting in the tops of doorways being flush with the face of the building. Door and window heads are elegantly finished with rounded fanlights, and the gable forms the principal façade, with a simple decorative dentil pediment on the gable end. The use of a pediment (a decorative triangular gable) is intentional in Federal architecture, referencing ancient Roman and Greek styles in order to symbolize democracy and a newly formed republic. Upper-level windows are quite intricately detailed with tracery and mullion patterning.

The interior is typically Federal in style, with the practical use of white walls and ceilings creating light and bright interior spaces, together with simple decoration. The ground floor is an open-plan space divided into three-by-two rows of simplified Doric columns, which form the support for the large open-plan hall on the upper floor. Although the detailing on the ground floor is utilitarian and pared back, the upper floor holds more ornate detailing, with moulded architraves, cornicing and dado rails.

The dentil cornicing, which is a simple repeated ornamentation in block form, refers back to the Roman and Greek Classical orders and is used to symbolize democracy and republican ideals.

JEFFERSONIAN 1790–1830

- **Palladian** design with a central core and symmetrical wings
- Entrances demarcated by a **portico** and **pediment**
- **Classical** orders and mouldings
- **Red brick** with white trim

MONTICELLO, CHARLOTTESVILLE

Architect: Thomas Jefferson
Construction started: 1769 (remodelling started in 1794)
Construction completed: 1809
Construction materials: Brick, stone and timber painted white
Area: 1020sq m (11,000sq ft)
Location: Charlottesville, Virginia, USA

The brilliant and self-taught Jefferson designed Monticello to outshine all other Virginia plantation houses and to pay homage to Andrea Palladio. Using Classical architecture as precedent, Jefferson set about reinventing and freeing American architecture from the constraints of English colonialism, to establish a new aesthetic for a democratic nation. Monticello was first constructed based on Palladio's writings, but after Jefferson travelled to Europe and experienced Classical architecture at first hand, he reinvented the house based on a deeper understanding of Classicism, transforming it into an architectural statement. His reconfiguration took on the elements of a Classical temple; for example, the main entrance is topped with a low Roman octagonal dome set on a pedimented Doric portico. Classical mouldings articulate the white-painted trims at high level and the sand-painted columns are set apart from the rest of the façade to give the impression of exaggerated grandeur. The construction of the dome structure proved that Classicism could be realized far from Europe. However, the dome actually plays little part internally, merely making up an attic room served by a steep, narrow staircase. The plan of the house follows the Classical central core, with two parallel wings forming a U-shaped courtyard building. The wings resemble long walkways and lead to gazebo structures in the landscape.

Jefferson cleverly employed natural ventilation, bringing ground-cooled air into the building at a low level and allowing warm air to rise within its large central hall space and leave through strategically placed high-level windows. This was a forward-thinking response to the climatic constraints found in the region.

GARDEN PAVILION WINDOW
A simple timber architrave, painted white, surrounds the sash window and frames the spectacular views out to the gardens of Monticello.

CLASSICAL ELEMENTS (ABOVE)
The south side of Monticello displays its Classical references, arched windows set in red brickwork, and sand-painted Doric columns supporting white-painted trim and Classical mouldings.

ORNATE MOULDINGS (RIGHT)
The view from the dining room into the tea room shows the heavily ornate timber mouldings painted white that decorate room openings, using variations on Classical proportioning to create a grand interior aesthetic.

KEY ARCHITECTURAL STYLES OF THE 19TH CENTURY

BRITISH REGENCY (1811–20)
The British Regency period was named after George, Prince Regent (later King George IV). Architecture during this period had links to Greek, Egyptian and Roman architecture, but the style is more correct than that of previous revivals. Façades resemble a marble finish, achieved by using stucco or painted plaster; this, combined with simple proportions and delicate ironwork, spoke of luxury for the nation's rising middle class.

BEAUX-ARTS (1830–1900)
Architectural design in Beaux-Arts style was established at the École des Beaux-Arts, the prestigious fine arts school established in Paris in the 17th century. It was inspired by French Neoclassical, Gothic and Renaissance elements used on city buildings at the time, and advocated Classical design, order and symmetry with grand ornamentation. Beaux-Arts style is more prevalent in the United States than in France.

VICTORIAN (1837–1901)
During the era of Queen Victoria, public buildings were designed to be extravagant, coated in fine decorative details such as tall finials and intricate window surrounds. With links to Gothic architecture, Victorian buildings were often asymmetrical, had castle-like towers and were covered in ornate motifs, resulting in a grandeur often celestial and church-like.

ART NOUVEAU (1890–1914)
The Art Nouveau movement began in the late 19th century in Europe as a reaction to the existing familiar architectural forms that heavily referenced historical styles. Driven by this need for a more free and innovative approach, buildings were no longer simply buildings, but could be expressed as artwork. Architects played with forms and materials, creating organic shapes and motifs with glass, metal, ceramics and stone, thus turning their architecture into sculpture.

ARTS AND CRAFTS (1880–1920)
Architecture in the mid-19th century was able to incorporate materials that were not always local. Originating in England and then spreading to Europe, the Arts and Crafts movement rebelled against this and advocated using only local materials and local craftsmanship. Previous eclectic styles and Classical proportions were also ignored by proponents of this quirky style. Internal structure such as beams were often celebrated and exposed with the occasional ornamental detail.

ANTONI GAUDÍ (1852–1926)
The highest concentration of Gaudí's work is in Barcelona, where he spent most of his life. Known as 'God's architect', Gaudí changed the path of architecture, which had previously been strongly influenced by Classical Roman and Greek architectural forms and styles. Gaudí's work was creatively original. He rarely drew floor plans and often created intricate three-dimensional models. By doing so, he was able to create complex façades concealed within delicate shapes.

PARKITECTURE (1872–1940)
During the late 19th century the Parkitecture movement began in American national parks, where there were limited materials and access was poor. Parkitecture encouraged the rejection of previously opulent styles and embraced a simpler, rustic approach. Influenced by the Arts and Crafts movement, native timber and stone were used to create buildings that blended into the surrounding landscape and aged with it as time passed.

19TH-CENTURY ARCHITECTURE

A time of massive social change, the 19th century also represents a time of war waged across Europe on a greater scale than ever before. It saw the peak of the Industrial Revolution, with progress in technology, transport and communications, and saw great advances in the materials used for construction.

In 1800, Great Britain united with Ireland to become the United Kingdom of Great Britain and Ireland. At the same time, the British Empire continued to expand, with colonies all over the world. The Napoleonic wars first began with Britain against France; however, the rest of Europe was quickly drawn in as France's victories and defeats created a shifting series of alliances that ended with Napoleon's final downfall at Waterloo in 1815. During and after the wars, the turmoil in France meant that agriculture suffered and industry stalled, taking years to recover. Spain, having allied with France, lost its colonies in the new world. Immense social changes took place throughout the century. Britain became the first European country to abolish slavery in 1834, and children aged under 10 were banned from working in mines in 1842.

Technology improved dramatically through the century, and by 1900 telephones and light bulbs were relatively commonplace. From the 1820s, cast iron was used in the structural framework of buildings. After 1880, construction using reliable steel frames became possible. In 1885, the Home Insurance Building in Chicago, United States, became the first tall building to have a structural steel frame.

ANTONI GAUDÍ'S SAGRADA FAMÍLIA
The Statue of Jesus Christ on the cross under the canopy of a ciborium in Gaudí's Sagrada Família has a backdrop of unique structural complexity.

BRITISH REGENCY 1811–1820

- **Symmetrical** façades and plans
- Classical **columns** onto **decorative** bands running along parapets
- **Unadorned** façades and Classical lines

PARK CRESCENT, LONDON

Architect: John Nash
Construction started: 1812
Construction completed: 1821
Construction materials: Masonry with stucco
Total length: 280m (918ft)
Location: London, United Kingdom

The Prince Regent commissioned John Nash to design a royal palace along with an urban masterplan surrounding it with parkland and a circus (a circular development) of grand townhouses to provide luxurious homes for his family and friends. Although the palace and the full circus were never built, a symmetrical royal crescent consisting of elegant stuccoed terraced houses forming the bottom half of the circus was realized, overlooking private gardens and quickly becoming London's most sought-after address. Portland Place divides the semi-circular crescent into equal halves and its inner face overlooks Regent's Park.

An encircling of the entire crescent in a colonnade of coupled Ionic columns at street level introduced an element of grandeur to the development. The colonnade is topped with a continuous sweeping stone balcony and balustrade. Depth is added to the façade by pushing the top floors back from the edge of the balcony to form a simple unadorned façade with Classical lines and tall sash windows, resulting in a sleek and shallow façade with minimal projections. The parapet has little embellishment other than a matching stone balustrade. The ends of the crescent are celebrated with a slight projection and low pediment detail. The façade was originally plastered with Roman cement or stucco in the pale honey colour of Bath stone; however, today it is painted white. The edges of the continuous basement level and bridge entry points to the houses are protected with a wrought iron railing with spear head detail and tassel patterning. The quiet symmetry, proportion and restrained elegance of Park Crescent provide an excellent example of British Regency style.

COUPLED COLUMNS
The colonnade of coupled Ionic columns is topped with a continuous sweeping stone balustrade demarcating the outer rim of the curved continuous balcony.

BEAUX-ARTS 1830–1900

- **Monumental** and **heavy** looking
- Flat or **hipped** roof
- Flat façades with **ornate patterns** or **scripture writings**
- **Rectangular, symmetrical** geometry with arches and decorative columns

SAINTE-GENEVIÈVE LIBRARY, PARIS

Architect: Henri Labrouste
Construction started: 1843
Construction completed: 1850
Construction materials: Limestone, glass and iron
Area: 1782sq m (19,182sq ft)
Location: Paris, France

This public and university library was designed in true Beaux-Arts style by Labrouste, a graduate of the famous École des Beaux-Arts. It inherited a collection of 12th-century books from the Abbey of Sainte-Geneviève and contains around two million documents.

The building was modelled on the Classical design of order and symmetry with grand and elaborate ornamentation. Its rectangular two-storey structure is simply monumental, with heavy stone proportioning. Large arched pilasters provide sensitive symmetry to the upper storey, framing arched windows and recessed flat stone panels of scribed carvings and ornate patterns. A leafy garland band above the first-floor windows is similar to ornamentation found on the nearby Panthéon and may reference the famous mausoleum. The roof is edged with a decorative stone parapet concealing a low-pitched roof behind. The lower level interior features flat arched ironwork between rectangular fluted columns, which support a reading room covering the entire first floor. The interior of the magnificent reading room, with its visible structural ironwork and ornately decorated stone arches, takes inspiration from Classical Roman architecture. This is one of the first important cultural buildings to use ironwork in a prominent manner, making it both visible and ornate. The internal iron structure consists of a slim spine of cast-iron Ionic columns running down the centre of the reading room, dividing it into identical aisles. The supporting ironwork comprises open iron arches carrying barrel vaults of plaster and reinforced with iron mesh. The use of intricate ironwork as a structural frame created a room that was unique at the time.

DECORATIVE WROUGHT IRON STRUCTURE
An ornate arched wrought iron structure holds a double-barrel vaulted roof. The wrought iron beams not only perform a structural function but a decorative one too.

VICTORIAN 1837–1901

- **Slate** roofing available due to better transport links
- Decorative roof **ridge** tiles
- **Simplified** motifs
- **Asymmetrical** designs
- Built with **larger bricks**
- Improvement in **comfort levels**

MANCHESTER TOWN HALL

Architect: Alfred Waterhouse
Construction started: 1868
Construction completed: 1877
Construction materials: Brick encased in Spinkwell stone (Yorkshire sandstone), concrete and iron
Height: 85m (280ft)
Location: Manchester, United Kingdom

Manchester Town Hall was built in the fashionable Neo-Gothic or 'High Victorian' style. Waterhouse won a competition to design the building, with a plan that cleverly incorporated ceremonial and working spaces into six storeys and maximized the tight triangular site. The building is demarcated by a perimeter corridor of cloister-like aesthetic linking offices and everyday functions.

The ceremonial features and spaces are centrally located, with two grand staircases connecting the Great Hall and entrances. The Great Hall is decorated with murals depicting the history of Manchester, while majestic chandeliers hang from a superbly painted ceiling made of panels showing different coats of arms. Gothic elements include low ribbed-vault ceilings and simple tall arched windows without carved decorations that are infilled with light-coloured glass. Technological advancements were integrated into the building, such as the warm air heating system and a ventilation system devised for drawing fresh air into the building, warming it and projecting it into the stairwells to ventilate the corridors. Gas pipes for lighting were concealed under the banister rails of the staircases and the building was designed to be fireproof using a combination of concrete and wrought iron beams.

The exterior shows a simplified Gothic style with limited carvings and uniform stonework, and is adorned with statues of important figures in Manchester's history. Interior decoration focused on cleanable surfaces and permanent colour; therefore public corridors were faced in terracotta with tile dados rather than plaster, ceilings were vaulted stone and there are washable marble mosaic floors.

CORBELLED STONE DENTIL WORK
Corbelled dentil detailing on the clock tower is in horizontal bands, with long, thin, deeply recessed windows below.

RIB-VAULTED CEILING (ABOVE)
The ceilings above the two main staircases are beautifully painted to exaggerate the ribs and draw one's eyes upwards while on the sweeping stairs.

SCULPTURE HALL (RIGHT)
The ground floor Sculpture Hall holds busts of the notable people who shaped Manchester. The room has an impressive groin-vaulted ceiling made from Bath stone.

GRAND STONE STAIRCASE (LEFT)
Two grand staircases lead up through the building to the landing outside the Great Hall. These stairs were designed with low risers so they could be used by women in Victorian dress. The walls of the staircases have tall arched windows allowing daylight to filter in, and the stairs are made of English, Scottish and Irish granite.

ART NOUVEAU 1890–1914

- **Curved** lines and **expressive** forms
- **Organic** motifs on façades
- **Extreme** in comparison to previous styles
- **Sumptuously coloured** tiles for bespoke patterns and mosaics

MUSEUM OF APPLIED ARTS, BUDAPEST

Architects: Ödön Lechner and Gyula Pártos
Construction started: 1893
Construction completed: 1896
Construction materials: Stone, iron, glazed bricks and tiles
Area: Approx. 5450sq m (58,660sq ft)
Location: Budapest, Hungary

Tired of the historical styles of Neo-Gothic, Neoclassicism and Neo-Palladianism, European architects took advantage of technological advances in materials to experiment with form and shape, creating exciting new architecture in Art Nouveau style. The Museum of Applied Arts takes reference from the Indo-Saracenic buildings and palaces of British India, where Indian Islamic and especially Mughal styles were interpreted by Victorian British architects. It is thought to be the first museum building in Europe to be designed in a new style, drawing on eastern, western and Hungarian vernacular architecture and using an unprecedented amount of colour on the exterior.

The tall, steeply pitched roofs and enormous dome are covered with bright green and gold glazed roof tiles in Hungarian style, made by Pécs Porcelain Factory. Walls are faced with glazed bricks and tiles in patterns resembling oriental rugs, and windows and railings are curvaceous and organic in shape. The porch façade is lined with red glazed bricks and has a patterned ceiling with flower motifs to resemble Mughal inlay marble work. Stairs to the entrance have balustrades in bright yellow majolica, a tin-glazed ceramic material. In contrast, everything inside the building is white, with the only colour on the stained-glass skylight over the central atrium space. Two-storey arcades with cusped (scalloped) arches, columns and openings influenced by Indian architecture surround the main internal space, which is roofed in iron and glass to flood it with daylight. Interiors are reminiscent of colonial-era British buildings. As a whole, the museum connects traditional forms with new organic shapes and colour to create a highly distinctive architecture.

MOSAIC PATTERNING
Column capitals are detailed with cusped edges influenced by Indian architecture to provide interest at the junction with the ceiling, which is decorated in a semi-Persian style.

THE ENTRANCE PORCH (BELOW)
The main entrance is a marvel of colour and ornately fantastical decoration. The walls are in glazed red brick and the organically shaped ceramic balustrade in bright yellow. The ceiling is patterned in intricate flower motifs, resembling Mughal inlay marble work.

ORNATE FORMS (RIGHT)
In the atrium one can see the use of curving forms inspired by Indian Islamic architecture, painted white to emphasize these shapes. Daylight enters the space from a skylight, providing an interior reminiscent of a colonial-era British building in India.

ARTS AND CRAFTS 1880–1920

- Evoked the ideas of independence and **rural** life
- Vast mix of materials
- **Exposed** internal structure
- Asymmetrical and **radical** design

RED HOUSE, BEXLEYHEATH

Architects: William Morris and Philip Webb
Construction started: 1859
Construction completed: 1860
Construction materials: Brick
Area: Approx. 636sq m (6,845sq ft)
Location: Southeast London, United Kingdom

Red House is an architecturally significant house built by William Morris, founder of the Arts and Crafts movement, and designed in collaboration with his friend Philip Webb. It was directly influenced by medieval buildings seen while travelling the Seine Valley, visible in the form of the turrets, steep overhanging roofs, prominent chimneys, cross gables, exposed beam ceilings, hipped dormer windows, pointed arches and conical-shaped well. These features epitomize the application of Gothic principles to domestic architecture without imitation.

The building's two-storey L-shaped plan allows the house to embrace the garden as part of the domestic realm and creates asymmetry. It was constructed in red brickwork with a steep red clay tile roof, all natural materials that were believed superior and healthier than industrially produced materials and sourced locally in Kent. The house lacks external ornamentation, instead favouring decorative features derived from function and construction methods, like arches over windows and the louvre in the open roof over the stair tower. The windows express the inner layout and functions of the house rather than fitting an external symmetry. They differ in size and shape, including narrow lancet windows, rectangular casements and round bulls-eye windows, providing an eclectic mix and supporting function over aesthetics. The architecture and the interior merge into a unified piece of design to create an atmosphere of domestic harmony and celebrating the ideas of art, craft and community that were so relevant to the Arts and Crafts movement. The interior and its furnishings were designed by Morris, his wife and friends, including the wall and ceiling paintings, the stained glass and the built-in furniture, following the 'medieval guild' ideal.

UPSTAIRS HALLWAY
The oak staircase has vertical, tapered newel posts, and the ceiling is painted in bold geometric patterns that are timeless and non-specific. This curvilinear design was painted by William Morris, Philip Webb and friends.

ANTONI GAUDÍ 1852–1926

- **Freedom** of **form** giving buildings a celestial presence
- **Organic** and sacred motifs
- Rich in **texture** and **colours**
- Developed his own **architectonic language**

SAGRADA FAMÍLIA, BARCELONA

Architect: Antoni Gaudí
Construction started: 1882
Construction completed: Anticipated 2026
Construction materials: Sandstone, granite, layers of flat bricks and reinforced concrete
Height: 172m (564ft)
Location: Barcelona, Spain

Sagrada Família (Basilica of the Holy Family) is an ongoing exercise in advancing construction technology and bridging the architectural time gap of 144 years. It was conceived on the principles of Gothic and Byzantine church architecture. However, Gaudí's design created a new and personal architectural style based on logical geometric structures and form but inspired by organic forms found in nature, with light and colour playing a vital role, to achieve symbiosis between form and Catholic iconography. Gaudí's design for this Basilica is otherworldly; the portion he completed speaks of an astounding ability to use geometry with organic architecture to produce a complex structure of awe-inspiring proportions and detail. The building will consist of 18 towers when complete. Its verticality symbolizes elevation heavenwards and is achieved by its external pyramidal design, pinnacles that reach for the sky, and its internal loftiness. Three monumental façades show Jesus' birth, his passion, death and resurrection, and his present and future glory.

Light and colour were critical in the design to express grandeur, and the interplay of light and shadow on the façades exaggerates the building's sheer immensity. Inside, the light is harmonious and emphasizes the plasticity of the nave. Gaudí viewed colour as the expression of life and used coloured Venetian stained glass and coloured bricks, stone and tiles. Structural columns branch out to suggest the idea of a forest within a temple. To reduce the roof loads, Gaudí sliced out pieces of the roof, inserting green and gold glass. He designed complex geometric forms to use structurally within the Basilica, resulting in a clever organic solution where light and colour were used to express grandeur.

THE SUFFERING JESUS
The sculpture of the suffering Jesus on the Passion Façade illustrates the last days of Jesus' life. The sculptural style is intended to emphasize the suffering that Jesus endured.

NAVE CEILIING (LEFT)
Gaudí designed the columns in the nave to resemble tree trunks with their capitals as branch nodes, as found in the natural world, with 'branches' supporting the roof. The ever-changing surfaces are the result of intersecting geometric forms.

THE PASSION FAÇADE (ABOVE)
The more recently built Passion Façade represents the passion and death of Jesus. It is therefore austere and seems relatively stripped back with its geometric-edged forms.

STAINED-GLASS RAINBOW (RIGHT)
In the lateral aisle, light is able to stream through the stained-glass windows.

PARKITECTURE 1872–1940

- Assertive **horizontal** lines
- Embracing **irregularity**
- **Avoiding** dainty materials
- Using **local stone** and **timber** and **local labour**
- **Scaling** the building to match its surroundings

CRATER LAKE LODGE

Architect: R.L. Hockenberry & Co and Crater Lake Company
Construction started: 1909
Construction completed: 1915
Construction materials: Stone and timber
Area: Approx. 3000sq m (32,700sq ft)
Location: Southern Oregon, USA

Crater Lake Lodge is an example of the architecture of the national parks of America. This movement towards creating buildings that blended into their surrounding natural landscape first started to appear before the formation of the National Park Service in 1916. The hotel was constructed right on the rim of a crater 300m (1000ft) above the lake. The vision was to create a visitor facility that didn't disturb the natural or historic surroundings, although this proved a difficult task. Locally sourced timber and stone was collected and transported long distances along poor roads, taking considerable time to get to site, and the harsh climate meant construction work was only possible for three months of the year. Simple traditional construction methods were used to create a visually appealing structure. The focus on local manual labour meant accurate construction was hard to achieve, giving the building an irregularity and asymmetry similar to those of the Arts and Crafts movement.

The lower storey is constructed in stone with large arched window openings. The upper storeys are clad in brown timber shingle and the roof in green shingle, interrupted by two rows of dormer windows and clipped gable ends. The hotel incorporated these local materials into the design in order to integrate the building with the site; however, due to the building's scale and location above the lake it remained relatively prominent. Even though Crater Lake Lodge set the ultimate standard for a national park lodge when it was built, the construction was unfortunately found to be inferior and subsequently it had to be relocated and rebuilt.

LOCAL MATERIALS
Construction using local stone, timber and labour was strongly advocated. The Lodge has been rebuilt in the same aesthetic as the original with exposed stonework and timber internally.

KEY ARCHITECTURAL STYLES OF THE 20TH CENTURY

EDWARDIAN (1901–10)
Emerging during the reign of King Edward VII, Edwardian architecture was very popular among the upcoming middle class. It is generally less ornate than Victorian styles and comfort in functionality became more readily available.

BAUHAUS (1919–33)
Bauhaus was a modern art school famous for its new approach to teaching by unifying all forms of arts and new technology. The movement favoured functionality over ornamentation and regular asymmetry.

ART DECO (1920–40)
The Art Deco movement, born in Paris, was influenced by Art Nouveau and Cubism. It is known for its glamour and use of expensive or new materials like chrome, ivory, plastic, animal skin and tortoiseshell. It became particularly popular in America.

FUTURIST (1908–41)
In 1909, Filippo Tommaso Marinetti wrote a manifesto proclaiming a transformation of the future and demanding social change. This inspired the Futurist movement, which focused on speed, technology and war.

FASCIST (1922–43)
Fascist architecture emulated the proportions and symmetry of ancient Rome and was designed to unify the people. Despite having pure architectural values, the style was used by Mussolini and Hitler for propaganda purposes.

PUEBLO REVIVAL (1920–30)
The Pueblo Revival style was influenced by Native American pueblo architecture. The pueblo style was coupled with Spanish colonial architecture to produce the Pueblo Revival style found predominantly in New Mexico and Arizona.

INTERNATIONAL STYLE (1926–76)
The International style is an important style developed in the 1920s and 30s with roots in Modernism. Traditional and bespoke was abandoned and simple geometric buildings with mass-produced materials resulted.

STALINIST (1933–55)
Under Stalin, the Soviet Union saw a massive regeneration plan put in place to transform cities. Architects took influences from Art Deco, Futurism and Gothic detail in their ornamentation. However, their purpose was mostly utilitarian and functional.

BRUTALIST (1950–75)
The term 'Brutalist' originated from Le Corbusier's French term *béton brut*, meaning raw concrete. This material is a key characteristic of Brutalist buildings, essential in creating their imposing nature and spartan confidence.

POSTMODERN (1960–2000)
Postmodernism emerged in the 1960s as a reaction to Modernist architecture. Buildings were designed with variety and personality that made them unique and, in many cases, highly visited tourist destinations.

HIGH TECH (1970 TO THE PRESENT)
Implemented by renowned architects Norman Foster and Richard Rogers, the High Tech movement was influenced by advances in engineering. Interiors were designed to be free from services such as ventilation, allowing space to be maximized and flexible to change.

20TH-CENTURY ARCHITECTURE

The first half of the 20th century was marked by rebellion, conflict and two world wars. By the end of the millennium, social and economic conditions in many parts of the globe had improved dramatically. Scientific and technological developments also changed the world forever. Architecture looked to the future rather than the styles of the past.

There was a revolution in the arts after World War I, in reaction to traditional values. Movements such as Cubism and Futurism allowed artists to express themselves freely and with little restraint. Social norms were increasingly questioned, leading to a new balance of relations between races, classes and genders. This period of social, economic and creative prosperity ended with the Wall Street Crash in 1929. The Great Depression that followed lasted until the outbreak of World War II in 1939, when global conflict helped to revive many national economies. With the restoration of relative peace after 1945, the west entered a new era of prosperity and technological innovation. By 1969, man had landed on the moon, and Concorde took its first transatlantic flight in 1973. In 1994, the Eurotunnel, one of the greatest engineering projects ever undertaken, linked Britain to the Continent for the first time since the Ice Age.

The 20th century is one of the most remarkable in history for its previously unparalleled technological advances and scientific discoveries. Some of the greatest innovations such as nuclear power, computers, aeroplanes, rockets, antibiotics, television and the internet, have had a profound influence on the human race both positively and negatively.

CITÉ RADIEUSE, MARSEILLE
Twentieth-century architecture is encapsulated in Le Corbusier's Cité Radieuse, with its progressive ideas, new construction methods and bold new solutions.

EDWARDIAN 1901–10

- **Red** bricks were prevalent
- Modern **architectural elements** like heating and damp-proof courses
- **Lighter** colours used
- Decorative patterns were **less complex**

MOSELEY ROAD BATHS, BIRMINGHAM

Architects: William Hale and Son
Construction started: 1895
Construction completed: 1907
Construction materials: Red brick, iron and terracotta
Area: Approx. 8180sq m (88,100sq ft)
Location: Balsall Heath, Birmingham, United Kingdom

The late 19th century witnessed the birth of the public bath house. Few homes were able to enjoy a water supply, so institutions such as Moseley Road Baths were built to improve public health. It provided a place where, for a nominal fee, one could go weekly to use a private washing room called a slipper bath. As such, Moseley Road Baths tells the story of British history, architecture and industrial heritage, symbolizing the rise of the working class and their introduction to leisure activities. It is an exceptional example of early 20th century public architecture and is the oldest Grade II listed swimming baths still operating in the UK.

The building's red brick and terracotta front façade is lavishly decorated and carries a large City Coat of Arms. Entrances into the building were segregated by both class and gender. In addition to the numerous slipper baths, the building contained two indoor swimming pools. The first-class Gala Pool has an intricate filigree ironwork arched structure spanning the entire width of the pool and spectators' galleries. A smaller second-class pool is also enclosed with attractive ironwork, yet is more modest in its detailing. The interiors of the building are a beautiful example of Edwardian style, with walls of glazed bricks in ivory, green and turquoise, floors of terrazzo (a composite material made of chips of coloured stone poured with a cementitious binder), lead windows of tinted glass, crafted wooden joinery, and state-of-the-art steam-heated drying racks.

GALA POOL
The architectural features of the building are impressive, both externally and internally. A three-sided spectators' gallery looks over the Gala Pool, which has a roof supported by pretty filigree ironwork exposed arches crossing the open-plan space.

BAUHAUS 1919–33

- **Mass production** and a mix of art and technology
- **No** unnecessary ornamentation
- **Minimalism** and simplicity
- **Geometric** purity
- Emphasizes ideas, **reform**, exploration and vitality

BAUHAUS, DESSAU

Architect: Walter Gropius
Construction started: 1925
Construction completed: 1926
Construction materials: Reinforced concrete, brick and glass curtain walling
Area: Approx. 23,280sq m (250,600sq ft)
Location: Dessau, Germany

The Bauhaus movement provided a unified vision with no distinction between form and function. Modern materials and industrial processes came to the forefront of design and were integral to the ethos of design. When Walter Gropius was commissioned to build a new art school providing a holistic approach to the creative disciplines, he seized the opportunity to design a bold and progressive building.

The asymmetrical pinwheel layout has interconnecting wings for different functions. The main elements of the complex are the glass-fronted three-storey workshop wing, the three-storey vocational school and the five-storey studio building. The three-storey blocks are connected by a two-storey administrative bridge, and the workshop wing and studio building are connected by a long single-storey building designed for the school's communal functions. The studio building contains 28 studio flats with balconies. Innovative construction methods were used, such as a load-bearing reinforced concrete and brick frame wrapped in large expanses of glazing, and flat roofs. In this way the school's structure is both revealed and celebrated. The façades are mostly white with dark-framed glazing, creating a striking aesthetic. These glazed curtain walls wrap around the corners, providing views into the building and highlighting its structure. They also ensure that large amounts of natural daylight enter the building and have mechanically opening windows for natural ventilation. The building encapsulated the idea of Bauhaus, with its interior fittings, furniture and lighting produced in workshops on site. It was alien and futuristic at the time of building, yet its influence is still seen all around us, from skyscrapers to graphic design and typography, to household items such as the tubular chair.

CURTAIN WALLING
Bauhaus Dessau's most striking feature is its glass curtain walling, which wraps around corners and provides views of the building's interiors and its supporting structure.

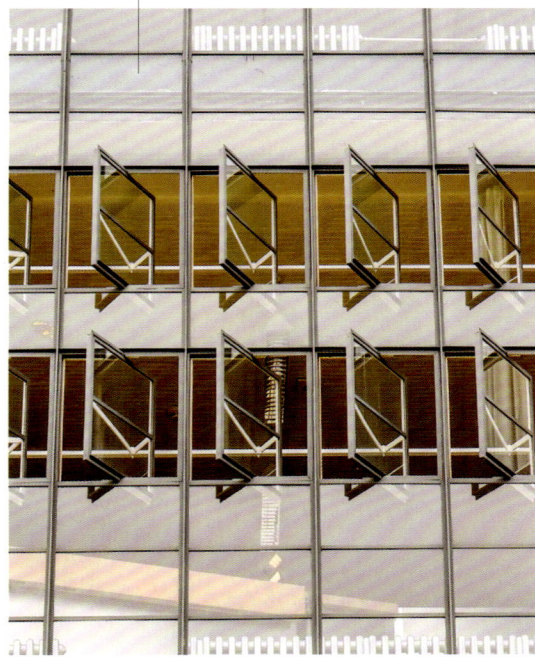

PINWHEEL PLAN (RIGHT)
The campus features an asymmetrical pinwheel plan with dedicated areas for teaching, an auditorium, offices, student housing and faculties distributed around three interconnecting wings.

STAIRCASE (LEFT)
The staircase in the five-storey studio building was used as a display area as well as for circulation. The glass walls provide good daylight, enabling these spaces to serve as places for students to meet and socialize.

STUDIO BUILDING (BOTTOM)
Uniformity, industrial materials and mass production are celebrated in the detailing on the façade of the dormitory accommodation of the studio building.

ART DECO 1920–40

- Daring, large-scale **geometric shapes**
- Associated with buildings of the **modern age**
- **Sleek** lines with **minimal ornamentation**
- Motifs had **Egyptian influences**

CHRYSLER BUILDING, NEW YORK

Architect: William Van Alen
Construction started: 1928
Construction completed: 1930
Construction materials: Steel frame infilled with concrete and metal cladding
Height: 319m (1047ft)
Location: New York, USA

The Chrysler Building was the first super-tall skyscraper influenced by the Art Deco era and the automobile age. The building plan rises in regular form, stepping in on one side at five stages. Its mid-section is uniform in plan then reduces to a Maltese cross, allowing for the square shaft to bend into a finial. Stainless steel is used extensively on flush window frames, for ornamentation, and for the crown and spire due to its non-rusting reflective properties, giving the illusion of the building vanishing into the sky. Gargoyles of Gothic influence decorate the corners of the building, resembling Chrysler radiator caps, Mercury's winged helmet and eagles. The frieze features hubcaps and fenders, symbolizing the Chrysler Corporation and expressing a visual signature of Art Deco design. The crown is composed of radiating terraced arches clad in stainless steel in a radiating sunburst pattern with inset triangular windows.

The interior holds some true decorative masterpieces of the Art Deco era. The extravagant triangular lobby has Moroccan red granite walls and flooring in yellow Siena travertine. Dim lighting gives a subdued quality, but the lighting fixtures are beautifully detailed in the style of the era and add an iconic feel to the space. Each elevator bank features a different design based on an abstract lotus pattern in metal with inlaid wooden veneers. The ceiling is painted with a mural paying homage to the aviation and automobile age in ochre and golden tones. The exterior and interior of the Chrysler Building, with its dramatic effects, elegant materials and striking ornamentation, make it an outstanding example of Art Deco style.

ELEVATOR DOORS
Metal elevator doors are covered with eight types of exotic timber. The Art Deco decorative work is influenced by Egyptian design and, when open, the lift car resembles an Art Deco room.

INTERIOR LOBBY (ABOVE)
The lobby space encapsulates the Art Deco era beautifully and is an architectural tribute to the automobile, with its Moroccan red marble walls, yellow travertine floors, chrome ornamentation and murals.

TERRACED CROWN (RIGHT)
Art Deco ornamentation is seen in the detailing of the terraced crown. It consists of seven radiating arches clad in stainless steel in a sunburst pattern, with triangular windows inserted along the arches.

EAGLE GARGOYLES (LEFT)
Designed to signify flight and exemplify the automobile and machine age, the building's gargoyles are reminiscent of the Chrysler car hood ornamentation.

FUTURIST 1908–41

- **Sharp** and precise lines
- Focused on **movement**, technology and science
- Embraced **new technology**
- **Small number** of buildings constructed in this controversial style

FIAT TAGLIERO SERVICE STATION, ASMARA

Architect: Giuseppe Pettazzi
Construction started: 1938
Construction completed: 1938
Construction materials: Reinforced concrete
Area: Approx. 897sq m (9658sq ft)
Location: Asmara, State of Eritrea, Africa

This Futurist-style service station with elements of Art Deco is located in Asmara, a city known for its well-preserved colonial Italian modernist architecture, built while it was part of Italian Eritrea. From 1890 to 1947, Eritrea was an Italian colony, part of its East Africa possessions. Italian architects designed hundreds of buildings in the region, including remarkable examples of Futurist construction. Asmara's architectural style was derived mainly from geometric simplicity and the aesthetic purity of rationalism. The most extraordinary structure to emerge from this was the Fiat Tagliero Service Station, an unashamed tribute to Futurism and its fascination with violence and modernity.

The service station was built on a major intersection, in a strategically important position linking Asmara to other Italian colonies by road to an international network of air travel. It was created as a tribute to the aeroplane, with a central tower providing functional space that resembles a cockpit with sleek wrap-around windows. The tower anchors a pair of breathtaking concrete wings spanning 15m (50ft) on each side. The Fiat Tagliero Service Station building embodies the idea of Futurism focusing on the illusion of speed with its aerodynamic shape and wing-like canopies. The wings stretch beyond what was conceived at the time to be possible with concrete structures, proving that technology was at the forefront of thinking. The creation of this seemingly impersonal and slightly brutal building hinted at war, violence and confrontation, summing up Futurism in one building.

'COCKPIT' TOWER
A central tower resembles a cockpit and anchors the huge cantilevered wings. A cashier's desk and shop are located on the ground floor; above these, office spaces address the street through sleek wrap-around windows.

FASCIST 1922–43

- Little decorative motif, except for carved **scriptures** and **slogans**
- **Monumental** commercial buildings
- **Simple** floor plans and bold design

PALAZZO DELLA CIVILTÀ ITALIANA, ROME

Architects: Giovanni Guerrini, Ernesto Bruno La Padula and Mario Romano
Construction started: 1938
Construction completed: 1943
Construction materials: Reinforced concrete with travertine marble cladding
Height/Area: 68m (223ft) and approx. 20,000sq m (215,300sq ft)
Location: EUR, Rome, Italy

The Palazzo Della Civiltà Italiana, known as the 'Square Colosseum', is an icon of Fascist architecture. It was designed as a centrepiece of EUR, the new area of Rome built under Mussolini for the 1942 World's Fair to celebrate Fascism, and as an ancient Roman structure re-envisaged for a modernized Rome. It was conceived as a box-shaped Colosseum with superimposed loggias on each façade formed as six rows of nine arches, with an extract from one of Mussolini's speeches inscribed all along the roof edge. The entire building, including the arches, vaulted ceiling and floors, is clad in travertine marble, characteristic of other local buildings and giving it a minimalist style typical of the brutal Modernism of the time. The rigid formality of the arcaded façade references the ancient Roman empire, yet the modern and dynamic form speaks of Futurism.

Located in a prominent position on a podium, the overall scale is imposing. The podium corners are marked by four equestrian sculptural groups representing mythical Greek heroes. 28 additional 3-metre-high (10ft) marble statues illustrating various industries and trades are located under each arch around the building's perimeter. Internally, all six storeys are bathed in light from the rows of 9-metre-tall (29ft) glass and bronze windows extending around all four façades. There are as many outdoor arched promenades as on any grand Renaissance palazzo and the exterior colonnade wraps around the entire building. The World's Fair was cancelled with the outbreak of war and Mussolini was later overthrown, so the palazzo was not occupied. However, in 2015, Rome-based fashion house Fendi made its headquarters there.

ARCHES
Travertine marble arches reminiscent of ancient Roman architecture, but devoid of any ornamentation, were a defining idea behind Fascist architecture.

PUEBLO REVIVAL 1920–30

- **Stepped** form to create multi-levels and many outdoor spaces
- **Flat** roofs with **tall parapet** walls
- **Rustic** finish
- **Simple geometry** internally and externally

NEW MEXICO MUSEUM OF ART, SANTA FE

Architect: Isaac Rapp
Construction started: 1917
Construction completed: 1917
Construction materials: Steel, concrete and stucco to resemble adobe (mud brick)
Area: Approx. 2441sq m (26,274sq ft)
Location: Santa Fe, New Mexico, USA

The New Mexico Museum of Art was inspired by the 300-year-old mission churches of Acoma and other *pueblos*, or Native American villages. It has the graceful simplicity of Pueblo Revival architecture and the appearance of having been created from earth. The main façade was modelled on the Mission of San Esteban del Rey at Acoma Pueblo, built between 1629 and 1641, and the layout is based on the original mission plan, with the museum's auditorium and entrance spaces positioned where the mission church and friary would have been. The museum surrounds a courtyard decorated with frescoes of traditional pueblo life. The portico wrapping around it is made of rough wooden supports, projecting painted corbels that support the structure above, and a *latillas* (peeled branch) ceiling resting on *vigas* (rough-hewn rafters), all traditional Spanish Colonial revival details.

Cement, plaster and a thick covering of stucco painted in earthy tones were used to mimic traditional adobe construction methods and to mask the modern brick and reinforced concrete structure. The building retains the visual characteristics of adobe, with rounded corners, irregular parapets and thick walls. The roof is flat and supported on wooden beams that typically project beyond the roof edges. Simple, decoratively carved wooden corbels are used to support the roofs. The interiors are equally detailed, and the auditorium resembles the mission church at Acoma's wooden ceiling, with large beams and curvaceous corbels. The museum is a fantastic and highly regarded example of Pueblo Revival architecture and is well known in the region for its combination of Native American and Spanish Colonial style.

PROJECTING WOODEN BEAMS
Pueblo Revival style features projecting wooden roof beams and hand-carved, stylized wooden corbels at the tops of columns and walls providing beam support where necessary.

INTERNATIONAL STYLE 1926–76

- Geometry is **modular** and **regular**
- **Façades** are designed **flush** with little relief
- **New technologies** in glass manufacturing allowed for larger panes of glass
- **Open interior** spaces

WILLIS TOWER, CHICAGO

Architects: Bruce Graham and Fazlur Rahman Khan of Skidmore, Owings & Merrill
Construction started: 1970
Construction completed: 1973
Construction materials: Bundled steel tube structural system, concrete and glass
Height: 443m (1453ft)
Location: Chicago, Illinois, USA

Willis Tower, with its bronze-tinted, glare-reducing glass façades framed in black aluminium, is a Chicago icon. Previously known as the Sears Tower, at 110 storeys it was the tallest structure in the world until the Petronas Towers were built in Kuala Lumpur. Its innovative structure and graceful design were unlike any other at the time and set a standard for future skyscrapers.

The building was extremely spacious for its height, with the lower floors taking up an entire city block before tapering as the building rises. The stepped-back design of the structure was stipulated by the client and by city regulations, resulting in a layout of very large office floors on lower levels and above them a variety of smaller floors for tenants. The building's proposed height was also a challenge, and a new solution was required to resist wind sway. Khan, the building's structural engineer, answered this by designing a 'bundled tube' system, which was a superstructure of nine interlocking square tubes of varying heights, each tube effectively a separate building. The tubes rise to varying heights and then stop, helping to break up wind force and allowing for the building to step back, creating an overall form that is truly iconic. This design made the tower structurally efficient and economical, while also providing open office space and uninterrupted city views. The structure is clad in aluminium and the façades in glass curtain walling. Laminated glass skydecks were added on the 99th and 103rd floor in 1974, allowing visitors to stand on and look through the glass floor to the street 412m (1353ft) below. Willis Tower was the last super-tall building constructed during the International style period and remains a remarkably bold and awe-inspiring interpretation of this style.

BRONZE TOWER
The Willis Tower steps in as it gets taller and is wrapped in black-framed bronze glazing, providing a shimmering and iconic form on the Chicago skyline.

STALINIST 1933–55

- **Utilitarian**
- Influenced by the **Brutalist** movement
- **Rigid** and **raw buildings** that lacked character
- **Symmetrical**
- Used as **propaganda** for Stalin's political views

MOSCOW STATE UNIVERSITY

Architect: Lev Rudnev
Construction started: 1949
Construction completed: 1953
Construction materials: Steel, brick and concrete
Height: 240m (787ft)
Location: Moscow, Russia

Stalinist architecture was intended to help turn the Soviet Union into a world power and was used to demonstrate its growth, prosperity and global status. Early attempts were deemed too plain and unsuccessful in promoting Stalin's ideas, so Classical references were added to buildings. Moscow State University is a true example of what Stalin was trying to achieve through architecture.

The university and its surrounding campus were designed with military precision and rigid planning to emphasize the idea of power. The buildings are massive and their size and symmetry were employed to show the Communist regime's might. As such, they incorporate the typically Gothic references of a strong sense of verticality, arches and mouldings. The main building consists of a very tall central tower with a pointed tip crowned in a Soviet star. It was the highest of seven Stalinist skyscrapers and is still the tallest educational building in the world. Ornamentation was applied to the building only where elements were to be celebrated, such as the entrance with its columns, elaborate capitals, frieze relief carvings and dentil cornicing, and the secondary lower towers holding oversized clocks, a thermometer and a barometer located on the four corners of the building. Two symmetrical wings of dormitories project from the central tower, stepping down in scale as one moves further away from the central core of the building. These wings are uniform, quite Brutalist, utilitarian and regimented in design. The Moscow State University building provides a monumental face to the city, its silhouette clearly visible from miles away. This truly dominant building remains a testament to Stalin's ambitions for Soviet architecture.

GIANT CLOCK
One of the towers on the Moscow State University is decorated with a giant clock, the biggest clock face in Moscow. The face is made in stainless steel and is 9m (30ft) in diameter. The minute hand is 4.1m (13ft) long and weighs 39kg (86lb).

BRUTALIST 1950–75

- A **fortress-like** appearance
- Critics argued buildings in this style were **impersonal** or **eyesores**
- **Experimentation** with shapes easily moulded with concrete

CITÉ RADIEUSE, MARSEILLE

Architect: Le Corbusier
Construction started: 1947
Construction completed: 1952
Construction materials: Off-shutter concrete
Height: 56m (184ft)
Location: Marseille, France

Cité Radieuse, or 'radiant city', was Swiss architect Le Corbusier's first project in his Modernist *Unité d'Habitation* design scheme for mass housing, and is one of the most influential Brutalist buildings of all time. Its human proportions, chunky pilotis (columns lifting the building off the ground) and interior 'streets' (or central access corridors) redefined high-density housing. Le Corbusier reimagined a city inside a Modernist 18-storey block, which would function as a 'machine' for the whole community to live in. The resulting Cité Radieuse is a self-contained concrete vessel accommodating a mix of uses, structured like a cruise liner and lifted off the ground to provide space for cars, bicycles and pedestrians. It consists of 337 apartments for up to 1600 residents and also houses shopping streets, a hotel and a communal rooftop terrace with a running track and children's paddling pool.

The structure was shuttered in textured wooden planks and *béton-brut* concrete was poured in, removing the need for structural steel and making the building cost effective and highly sculptural. It also created the style's emblematic punctured concrete surfaces. The elevations consist of a series of balconies and deep-set windows that reveal the concrete structure of the building. Opposites are expressed in the contrast of rough against smooth and dull concrete against brightly coloured balcony recesses. Internally, most flats interlock around a central access corridor or 'street', streamlining circulation. Despite the rigid layout and thick soundproof concrete walls limiting the flexibility to reconfigure internal spaces, and its strong Brutalist form, Cité Radieuse proved a successful model and remains very popular with its mostly professional residents.

CONCRETE STAIRWAY
External concrete stairs made from off-shutter concrete turn into a sculptural form that requires no dressing or decoration and is purely functional yet with a beautiful form.

POSTMODERN 1960–2000

- **Little continuity** among buildings other than values and reasoning
- Engineering pushed to create **expressive forms**
- Asymmetric, unstable-looking design with a **sporadic** nature

BERLIN PHILHARMONIE

Architect: Hans Scharoun
Construction started: 1960
Construction completed: 1963
Construction materials: Concrete and anodized aluminium cladding
Auditorium height: 22m (72ft)
Location: Berlin, Germany

The Berlin Philharmonic concert hall illustrates the typical qualities of Postmodernism, such as the return of wit, ornament and reference, along with the rejection of the strict rules of Modernism. Various styles collide, the eclectic tent-like roof shapes create brightly coloured sweeping forms, there is both structural and material variety, and the building has an organic form rather than a Modernist orthogonal shape. This iconic building is a deviation from Modernist thinking, with its asymmetrical shape and appearance of a golden draped tent.

The building comprises two venues: a large 2440-seat auditorium and a smaller chamber music hall with 1180 seats, linked with a rich, fragmented and eclectic lobby space. Both internally and externally, the building rejects the simplicity of Modernism, rectangular organization and symmetry, making up its own design rules. Its shape is derived from the principles and demands of acoustics. The main auditorium space is shaped to project sound in all directions with seating in offset terraces to maximize sound performance, while the angular ceiling over the auditorium space heightens rhythmic sound. The insertion of a central stage surrounded by the audience was innovative at the time, placing music at the centre of the design both metaphorically and physically. The building's external appearance is secondary to the requirements of the interior. Even so, the façade is distinctly recognizable due to its gold-anodized aluminium cladding, which provides material variety to the concrete structure. The exterior façades are dynamic and create a dialogue with their surroundings. The Berlin Philharmonie exemplifies Postmodernist ideas executed to a highly technical specification, creating genuinely iconic architecture.

COMPOSITIONS IN GLASS
Circular stained-glass elements designed by Alexander Camaro have been inserted into the exterior concrete walls to provide a coloured light effect to the interior, enhancing the festive character of the building.

BROKEN FORM (ABOVE)
Non-orthogonal sculptural shapes and broken form are highlighted in gold when lit at night.

FOYER SPACE (RIGHT)
Colourful mosaic works inspired by Johann Sebastian Bach and designed by Erich F. Reuter have been inserted into the natural stone floors in the foyer space.

DRAPED AUDITORIUM (FAR RIGHT)
Music is placed at the centre and surrounded by an audience. Sounds resonate off the carefully draped and fragmented enclosure to provide perfect rhythm and acoustic quality. The hall was envisaged by the architect as a valley, with the orchestra situated at the valley floor and the audience surrounding it in ascending terraced 'vineyards'.

HIGH TECH 1970–

- Celebrates **exposed** structures
- **Services uncovered**, such as ventilation and heating units
- Prefabricated elements
- Roots in **Brutalism** and **Postmodernism**

LLOYD'S BUILDING, LONDON

Architect: Richard Rogers Partnership
Construction started: 1978
Construction completed: 1986
Construction materials: Concrete, stainless steel and glass
Height: 88m (289ft)
Location: London, United Kingdom

High Tech architecture, also known as Structural Expressionism, is a late modern architectural style that emerged in the 1970s and brought high-tech industry and technology into the building world. Richard Rogers had just completed the Centre Pompidou in Paris when he was commissioned to design the Lloyd's building. Like the Pompidou, it was designed 'inside out'. All services were removed from the interior and placed in zones on the exterior of the building, freeing up interior space to accommodate changing business functions. It also meant that the services are more easily accessed for maintenance and retrofit with no disruption of business functions internally.

The building consists of three main towers, each with its own service tower, located around a colossal rectilinear atrium space. Each floor has galleries overlooking this atrium, lit from above through a glass barrel-vaulted roof. Rising through the lower levels of the atrium is a series of escalators linking the floors and providing dynamism to the space. Rogers proposed a building where the dealing room could expand and contract by using galleries around a central atrium with movable partitions, resulting in a flexible building that could adapt to changes in the market. The façade appears as a kit of parts, and the entire building is wrapped in stainless steel, giving it a machine-like quality and High Tech character. The sleek metal façade set against the exposed services demonstrates technological advancements in construction and expresses the building's functionality. The Lloyd's building brought a High Tech architectural aesthetic to London's historic financial district and successfully demonstrated that modern buildings, when well considered, can sit comfortably within any built environment.

STAINLESS STEEL AND GLASS CANOPY
The main entrance at the base of the Lloyd's building's Tower One is identifiable by the grand cantilevered canopy with a barrel-vaulted glazed profile echoing the main atrium roof inside the building.

ARCHITECTURAL MASTERS OF THE 20TH CENTURY

FRANK LLOYD WRIGHT (1867–1959)
Frank Lloyd Wright was an American architect, interior designer, author and professor who designed more than 1114 structures. Wright believed in organic architecture and created some of the most innovative spaces in the United States.

LUDWIG MIES VAN DER ROHE (1886–1969)
Known as Mies, this German-American architect established the International style as the definitive architectural language of North American post-war Modernism. He worked with stone, chrome, bronze and brick and his buildings were noted for their fine craftsmanship, along with their industrial methods of construction.

LE CORBUSIER (1887–1965)
Charles-Édouard Jeanneret, known as Le Corbusier, was a Swiss-French designer who formulated the ideas behind a truly modern architecture during the interwar period. His ideas about immense, rationalized, zoned and industrially constructed cities both shocked and seduced a global audience.

I.M. PEI (1917–)
This Chinese-American architect studied the work of Le Corbusier and other pioneers of modern architecture. His most famous pieces, such as the Louvre Pyramid, are predominantly made from glass and steel and follow strict rules of geometry.

OSCAR NIEMEYER (1907–2012)
The award-winning Brazilian architect Oscar Niemeyer Soares Filho was a pioneer in the modern architecture movement and designed many of the civic buildings in Brazil. With roots in International architecture, Niemeyer used abstract forms to create fluid shapes using materials such as concrete and steel.

FRANK O. GEHRY (1929–)
The Canadian-American toys with gravity, creating buildings that are sculptural pieces made from ribbons of steel, concrete panels and glass. Gehry uses elements of Deconstructivism and Futurism and transforms buildings into powerful works of art.

ÁLVARO SIZA (1933–)
Portuguese architect Siza is known for his *laissez-faire* attitude and his buildings mirror this with their effortless, cool appeal. Siza focuses on the intimacy of architecture, using uninterrupted lines and simplistic design to create modern, endearing forms.

NORMAN FOSTER (1935–)
Foster's radical, modern approach to architecture, use of large-scale radial geometry and environmental consideration is expressed through the High Tech and Sustainable architecture movements. The British architect's work brings a sense of humanity to commercial environments.

ZAHA HADID (1950–2016)
An Iraqi-British architect and the first woman to receive the Pritzker Architecture Prize in 2004, Hadid never followed a style or movement, yet her early work had an essence of Brutalism. Her more recent work is defined by delicate and lightweight materials that create structures and spaces with fluid, futuristic qualities.

SANTIAGO CALATRAVA (1951–)
With a career in structural design, engineering, sculpture and painting as well as architecture, the Spaniard Calatrava uses all his professional skills to create profound gravity-defying structures. His work is often described as Neo-Futuristic; some reference is also made to Gothic ornamental elements.

MASTERS OF THE 20TH CENTURY

The pioneers of Modernist architecture created the most influential design style of the 20th century. With an understated approach, simplistic design and a willingness to be structurally innovative, the ten design disciples detailed here were part of a larger cohort changing the way we live and work.

The machine age brought about a revolution in materials in the 20th century where iron, glass and concrete became more commonly used to create fluid forms. The purity of design realized with these raw materials was a rebellion against the previous Neoclassical styles. Each of the architects in this chapter has their own distinctive, easily recognizable style, yet they all fall under the same Modernist umbrella.

The Modernist movement, combined with technological advancements, improved lifestyles. Architects are more aware now than ever before of the social and environmental impact of their buildings. Recent Modernist architecture has allowed architects to create gravity-defying, monolithic forms that are sensitive to nature, incorporating, for example, renewable energy sources and sustainable materials.

These masters of architecture took a holistic approach to design. Not only did they design the building, they oversaw the contents, too, from Le Corbusier's artwork, Frank Lloyd Wright's furniture and even Zaha Hadid's 'futureskin' sportswear. As a woman, Zaha Hadid also had a huge influence on what is a male-dominated industry. She was the first woman to win the prestigious Pritzker Prize in 2004, as well as the Stirling Prize and other high-profile awards.

MASTERFUL DESIGN
Masters of the 20th century have created inspiring and ground-breaking architecture, such as Calatrava's Oriente Station, forging the way forward.

FRANK LLOYD WRIGHT 1867–1959

- **Organic** architecture, designed from the inside out
- Pushed **materials** often to the brink of structural failure
- Democratic **design**, architecture for everyman
- **Occupant-driven** design with form following function

TALIESIN WEST, SCOTTSDALE

Architect: Frank Lloyd Wright
Construction started: 1937
Construction completed: 1959
Construction materials: Desert stone, sand, concrete and redwood timber
Area: 2.5sq km (0.97sq miles)
Location: Scottsdale, Arizona, USA

Taliesin West was Frank Lloyd Wright's winter home and school of architecture in the desert from 1937 until his death. First conceptualized in 1927 to escape the harsh winters of the Midwest, Arizona's arid desert climate proved to be a place that could inspire Wright and his apprentices. Organic architecture to Wright was not about shape or form, but was based on the belief that architecture has an essential connection with both its site and time, making the relationship of building to landscape paramount.

The complex of buildings is made up of long, low, sweeping lines, uptilting roof lines and horizontal planes that keep the buildings close to the ground to ensure natural ventilation and protection from the intense desert sun. Buildings are connected through terraces, gardens and pools, and resemble spiky desert plants, resulting in a harmonious co-existence with the desert environment. Surface patterning achieved through clever use of natural materials gives the structures a resemblance to the natural camouflage of desert animals. The most significant use of material for the building is the desert stone found on site and used in the formwork concrete walls. Using redwood shuttering, the flat face of stones was directed outwards and the spaces between stones infilled with concrete, creating the unusual large stone walls and structural elements of the house. Redwood timber was used for the roof structure, interior elements and the studio's façade cladding. The rich red hue, along with the sandy tones of the concrete and stone, blends the house into the surrounding landscape. The relationship of inside to outside is seamless and the building is very much of the desert.

GEOMETRIC STRUCTURE
Wright's strong use of geometric form likens the building to spiky desert plants, while the use of natural materials and a low form root the building into the landscape.

LUDWIG MIES VAN DER ROHE 1886–1969

- **Mies** pioneered the **modern architecture** movement
- Built **'skin and bones'** designs
- **Seamless** interior and exterior spaces
- Minimal privacy with **maximum** glass panels

SEAGRAM BUILDING, NEW YORK CITY

Architect: Ludwig Mies van der Rohe
Construction started: 1954
Construction completed: 1958
Construction materials: Reinforced concrete, bronze and glass
Height: 157m (515ft)
Location: New York, USA

The Seagram Building represents Mies's definitive statement on the form of the skyscraper. He had been working on the idea since the early 1920s, but this was the first office tower commission he was able to build and his first in New York. The building has a sculptural quality that is manifested in two ways. First, he used bronze, a material more usually employed for honorific exterior sculpture. Second, he set it back from the street behind an open plaza, giving his design space to be appreciated and underlining the sense of the skyscraper as sculpture, via its luxurious and precisely geometric form. The Seagram Building's design is somewhat understated. Mies chose to enclose the fireproof concrete-clad steel frame in a metal casing, and then to emphasize each vertical spandrel (or horizontal panel between each line of windows) with an ornamental I-beam rising the entire height of the building to reinforce the sense of verticality. Significantly, these I-beams and the exterior structure are made of bronze, which gives the structure a dark tone, almost like a looming monolith. The building used a massive 1500 tons (1360 tonnes) of bronze, which at the time made it one of the most expensive skyscrapers ever built.

Mies's strategy with the plaza represented a new concept of corporate modern identity, where the company gifted the public a useful space within its dedicated building plot that also opens the street below to more natural light. It was also his way of satisfying New York's zoning law, which insisted that skyscrapers be set back from the street once they reached a certain height, to allow sunlight to filter down.

EXTRUDED BRONZE CURTAIN WALLING
The façade holds the largest I-beams ever extruded. The curtain wall has extruded architectural bronze I-beam mullions and spandrels with pink-grey, heat-resistant and glare-resistant glass in storey-high bronze frames.

LE CORBUSIER 1887–1965

- **International** style, **Modernist** movement
- Designed with **space**, **light** and **order**
- The **free plan** allowed maximum flexibility
- **Ribbon windows** highlight the link to nature

VILLA SAVOYE, POISSY

Architect: Le Corbusier
Construction started: 1929
Construction completed: 1931
Construction materials: Reinforced concrete and masonry units
Height: 9.4m (30.8ft)
Location: Poissy, near Paris, France

Villa Savoye is arguably Le Corbusier's most renowned work, and a prime example of Modernist architecture. It strongly conforms to his developed five-point system for new architecture; pilotis, open-plan interiors, façade free from structural constraints, ribbon windows and roof gardens. The sleek white planar geometry of the upper building's volume, with its elongated ribbon windows letting in light and reinforcing the planar quality of the walls, is supported by a series of pilotis, or narrow columns. These raise the building off the ground, allowing for circulation below, while a curved glazed entrance topped with a solarium brings nature into the urban setting. The building is designed as a direct response to the path of the sun and the views from the interior. The layout, form and positioning of the circulation has been derived using the golden ratio.

The building was revolutionary in that the use of reinforced concrete meant that fewer load-bearing walls were required internally, resulting in open-plan space that was flexible to be used in any manner. The building is both a functional house and a Modernist sculpture, elegantly merging form and function. The floating box form of the building embodies Le Corbusier's concept of style, along with the careful consideration of arrival at the building and how one moves through it, and the use of proportion, all connecting the building back to Classicism. At the same time, its clean simplicity and its use of concrete reference the precisely calibrated works of engineering so admired by the architect. Villa Savoye represents Le Corbusier's reconception of the very nature of architecture, and his attempt to express a timeless Classicism through the language of architectural Modernism.

FAÇADE FREE FROM STRUCTURE
As part of Le Corbusier's five-point system used in his designs, the free façade is most important. Here the glass façade runs past the structural column and concrete roof beam to provide two separate elements.

CONCRETE SPIRAL STAIRCASE (LEFT)
The interior is organized around a multi-storey, sensuously curved staircase that leads the visitor on a gently curving path through a predominantly rectilinear building.

MASTER BATHROOM (RIGHT)
A curvaceous reclining shape in small grey tiles frames the end of the rectilinear bath, which is fitted out in contrasting blue tiles. The feature is reminiscent of the Turkish baths Le Corbusier would have seen while travelling.

EXTERIOR RAMP (BOTTOM)
An exterior ramp carries visitors from the terrace to the solarium. White concrete walls guard the ramp and provide a sleek ocean liner aesthetic.

I.M. PEI 1917–

- **International style**, Modernist movement
- **Simple forms** and honest materials
- Merging traditional **Chinese architecture** with **modern design**

SUZHOU MUSEUM

Architect: I.M. Pei with Pei Partnership Architects
Construction started: 2002
Construction completed: 2006
Construction materials: Black granite and white stucco
Area: 2,200sq m (23,700sq ft)
Location: Suzhou, Jiangsu, China

Built in 2002–06 in Pei's home town, Suzhou Museum combines the traditional geometry of the surrounding buildings with the visual elements that defined his previous work. Pei is regarded as the last surviving pioneer of modern architecture and, as his final project, the museum is a paramount piece within the Modernist movement.

The edges of each form are lined in black granite to define and enhance the squares, rectangles and pyramids that fold together to make the overall structure. The harmonious rectangular layout wraps around the main water garden, blending both the building and landscape into one. The main line of symmetry running down the middle of the site, the geometric language and the highlighted edges are all elements used in both modern and traditional Chinese architecture, and they are executed poetically by Pei. However, strict height restrictions in China meant the museum had to be built to a modest size, to ensure surrounding historic buildings were not compromised.

Inside the museum, the use of milky glass creates a haze that transforms its monumental areas into intimate gallery spaces. Pei enriched the interior of the building with handcrafted ceramics and elements of jade and bronze that mirror the expensive artwork. Modulated shapes leading up to the sloping roof create dynamic light beams inside, originating from the traditional Suzhou folded roofs. Now a UNESCO World Heritage Site, the museum is a destination not only for its contents, but also for its architecture. It represents the ideas of contrast and, ironically, cohesion, with its conflicting materials and gentle mix of architectural styles.

FORMS ON WATER
Squares, rectangles and pyramids wrap around the water features, creating a tranquil complex of building forms that symbolize the Chinese culture yet were executed using modern methods.

OSCAR NIEMEYER 1907–2012

- Mixed Baroque and modern architecture to form a **new Brazilian** architecture
- Designs had intense **geometry** and **symmetry**
- Use of **daring abstract forms** and curves
- Worked on over **600** projects

CATHEDRAL OF BRASÍLIA

Architect: Oscar Niemeyer
Construction started: 1958
Construction completed: 1970
Construction materials: Concrete, fibreglass and stained glass
Height: 40m (131ft)
Location: Brasília, Brazil

The Cathedral of Brasília was designed to have the same pure form from all perspectives. It is one of the city's most famous and instantly recognizable buildings due to its concrete hyperboloid structure, which represents two hands reaching for the heavens. The cathedral is monumental in size at around 60m (197ft) in diameter and has a capacity of up to 4000 people. Its hourglass shape was achieved with 16 concrete columns that curve inwards to evoke the image of a crown of thorns. A shallow reflection pool surrounds the cathedral, providing a passive cooling effect while adding to its majesty. The impressive structure emphasizes the importance of the Roman Catholic Church without the need for Gothic ornamentation; however, there are hints of this in the bronze sculptures of evangelists alongside.

Internally, the light filtering through the stained-glass windows suspended between the concrete fingers creates an inspiring and uplifting atmosphere, providing a contemporary take on historical biblical stained glass. The theatrics and grandeur often found in the more traditional Gothic churches are replicated here in a simplified and contemporary manner. An underground entrance leads visitors into the luminous holy space, where the concrete 'hands' encourage the eye heavenwards.

Now an iconic symbol of Brasília, the cathedral is still used for Roman Catholic services and is also open to the public. By pushing the limits of engineering, using a simple concept and hints of a Gothic past, Niemeyer created the perfect example of awe-inspiring modern religious architecture that pays homage to structural expressionism and monumental architecture.

CONCRETE HYPERBOLOID STRUCTURE
The concrete structure represents two hands reaching for the heavens in a futuristic and symbolic fashion.

FRANK O. GEHRY 1929–

- Elements of **deconstructivism** and **Futurist**
- **Free-flowing** sculptural forms
- Experimental **poetic** façades

GUGGENHEIM MUSEUM BILBAO

Architect: Frank O. Gehry
Construction started: 1993
Construction completed: 1997
Construction materials: Limestone, glass and titanium
Height: Hall is 50m (164ft)
Location: Bilbao, Spain

The Guggenheim Foundation first made architectural history in 1959 with the opening of Frank Lloyd Wright's Guggenheim Museum in New York. Ground-breaking architecture was used to create an iconic building that is a work of art and as important as the art it holds. The Guggenheim Foundation was approached by the Basque Government in 1991 to commission their own Guggenheim Museum in Bilbao for Spanish and other contemporary art on the banks of the Nervion River. Like the original Guggenheim, this building is hailed as one of the most admired pieces of architecture of its time.

Frank Gehry was tasked with designing a museum that was to be as daring and innovative as possible, the difference being in its execution – this time technology had advanced and the curves of the exterior of the building appear random and are used to catch and reflect the light in different ways. Its free-form, organic shape and seeming frivolity have made it iconic. Rigid traditional materials such as glass and limestone have been teamed with titanium, a modern material that can be bent in organic and sensuous shapes, to provide a modern fluid take on deconstructivism. The complex shapes, curvaceous nature and twisted forms were designed using three-dimensional digital modelling. Today this has become standard in architecture, but it was quite revolutionary at the time. Internally, a parallel can be drawn with the original Guggenheim Museum. It is designed around a large interior atrium that is filled with daylight. However, this museum has views out of the building over the Bilbao Estuary rather than being completely internalized.

TITANIUM CLADDING
The titanium panels are formed into organic and sensuous shapes – a contemporary take on deconstructivism.

ATRIUM (ABOVE)
When entering the building there are many awe-inspiring, tall, fragmented and chaotic spaces that are flooded with light, creating the perfect background for artwork.

SCULPTURAL FORM (LEFT)
The sculptural building form demands attention. The building is set within public space, allowing the viewer to appreciate the building and its many changing façades from different angles.

ÁLVARO SIZA 1933–

- Has **creative control** over every project
- Poetic Modernist, favoured **modest**, simple forms of architecture
- Highlights and exaggerates the **juxtaposition** of **light and dark**

LLOBREGAT SPORTS CENTRE, BARCELONA

Architect: Álvaro Siza
Construction started: 2005
Construction completed: 2005
Construction materials: In-situ concrete (concrete structure poured on site)
Area: 40,000sq m (430,500sq ft)
Location: Cornellà, Barcelona, Spain

Siza designed this simple structure as an oasis of effortless curves set within the landscape. Part of a sports park development, the Llobregat Sports Centre was constructed on a flat piece of land west of central Barcelona. The centre is made up of four connecting masses, including a sports hall and swimming pool, and is constructed in white concrete. Its curved roof line echoes the Cornellà hills in the background, simulating the idea of a rolling landform, and by wrapping large ramps around the sports centre Siza created a sense of climbing a terrain. The centre's stark white, smooth walls appear cold at first but are softened through the clever placement of skylights allowing in the sun.

Inside the building, Siza simplified the traditional dado rail by painting the floor and lower part of the walls a dark grey, which enhances the double height spaces and makes them more intimate. High-level windows are used throughout to frame the Cornella hills, but the entrance has an internalized view of the pool at the end of the sports centre. The indoor pool area has an elliptical domed roof with 62 circle skylights; when these spots of light hit the water they reflect onto the walls and pool surface, playfully turning the space into a ball of light. The Llobregat Sports Centre is a key example of Siza's effortless-seeming style and his modern design. Using monolithic materials (large expanses of one material, in this case concrete), simple and beautiful forms, and direct and reflected light, a building that could be construed as having elements of Brutalism was moulded into a poetic, sculptural form set in the landscape.

SCULPTURAL FORM
Siza created buildings with sculptural forms that are constantly evolving through the interplay of shadow and light.

NORMAN FOSTER 1935–

- **Monumental** scales and truth to material
- **Structural Expressionism** and ecological design
- Socially **responsive** architecture and public spaces
- **Cutting-edge** technology for simple, clean designs

30 ST MARY AXE, LONDON

Architects: Foster & Partners and Arup Group
Construction started: 2001
Construction completed: 2003
Construction materials: Steel and glass
Height: 180m (591ft)
Location: 30 St Mary Axe, City of London, United Kingdom

When the concept sketches for 30 St Mary Axe were publicized, critics were wary of the impact of such a modern shape on the skyline. However, 'The Gherkin', as the building is commonly known, is now a well-integrated and iconic landmark in the London cityscape. The building sits within a tight, narrow city grid yet does not feel over-imposing. At ground level its sheer height and mass is concealed by a cleverly shaped tower that widens as the building gets taller, then tapers to its apex. This socially responsive approach to architectural design reduces the feeling of the building being overbearing at street level, while opening it up at ground floor to spill out onto a plaza creates a public urban space. Creating an energy-efficient high-rise building was another driving concept, and this project was the UK's first commercial skyscraper to explore the use of environmentally progressive techniques. Atriums allow natural ventilation and daylight to penetrate the building, making internal working spaces more comfortable and promoting wellbeing.

Building engineers Arup used cutting-edge technology to design a triangulated perimeter structure that provides enough stiffness to enable column-free internal floor space and a fully glazed building skin. As tall buildings of this nature are subject to high wind loads and deflection, Arup also designed the building with increasing stiffness to stop it swaying. The remarkable overall curved shape of the building is formed from this triangulated perimeter structure holding each glazed unit. Although these units are all flat panes of glass, the overall illusion is of curved glass however, the only truly curved glazing on the building is the lens-shaped cap that crowns it.

ATRIUM SPACES
Environmental considerations were expressed every six floors, with an open atrium six floors high allowing for natural ventilation and sunlight to pass deep into the building. Every six floors the plan twists to shift the next atrium around the building.

ZAHA HADID 1950–2016

- **Relationship** between plan, section and elevation
- Extreme, asymmetrical, **free-flowing** forms
- **Minimalist** materials
- Uses arches and **curves**
- Flexible and **curious** forms

LONDON AQUATICS CENTRE

Architects: Zaha Hadid and Arup Group
Construction started: 2008
Construction completed: 2011
Construction materials: Steel, aluminium and glass
Area: 12,800sq m (137,800sq ft)
Location: Olympic Park, London, United Kingdom

The London Aquatics Centre was originally designed in 2004 by Dame Zaha Hadid for a competition, before London won the bid to hold the 2012 Olympic and Paralympic Games, and then adapted to fit Olympic requirements, with two 50-m (164-ft) pools, a 25-m (82-ft) diving board and 17,500 seats. Inspired by the fluidity and movement of a wave, it became one of the most recognizable buildings of the Games and inspired many new builds, such as the Dollan Aqua Centre in Scotland.

With roots in the Brutalist and Futurist movements, the building's gravity-defying design makes it appear almost otherworldly. The main design focus is the parabolic arch sitting at its centre, which is made from steel and aluminium. Using three-dimensional printers, Hadid and her team were able to create intricate, concrete-finished geometric patterns on the ceilings that, when lit up, hint at patterns seen in the Islamic architecture movement. The strict time constraints on the project meant it mainly used pre-cast concrete to speed up construction. After the London Olympics, the building was extensively remodelled so it could be used efficiently by the public and for international aquatic events. Thousands of temporary spectator seats were recycled and the wings on either side of the building were removed and replaced with glass to let natural light enter, a feature of Hadid's original design. One of the key drivers for the design was the need for Olympic buildings to leave a legacy benefiting the local area and especially young people, and Hadid contributed to this aim by using high-tech engineering, simple materials and a natural concept.

CURVACEOUS CEILING
Internally, the ceiling is clad in sustainable timber battens following the curves of the concrete structure, which act to soften the otherwise very industrial interior.

WAVE ROOF (ABOVE)
The building's wave-like roof is reflected in the water of the adjacent river. The roof is 160m (525ft) long and approximately 80m (262ft) wide, weighing 3000 tonnes (2952 tons) and constructed in aluminium and steel.

POOLS (RIGHT)
A total of 462 tonnes (455 tons) of concrete was used for the seamless diving platforms, and the floor of the pool was designed to rise and fall, changing the depth of the water for different Olympic events.

SANTIAGO CALATRAVA 1951–

- **Minimalist,** stark white design
- Hypnotic and **fluid** structures
- Blends both **architecture** and **engineering**
- Designs reflect the **natural world**

LISBON ORIENTE STATION

Architect: Santiago Calatrava
Construction started: 1995
Construction completed: 1998
Construction materials: Mixed masonry, limestone, timber, wrought and cast iron
Height: 25m (82ft)
Location: Lisbon, Portugal

In 1992, Calatrava won the bid to design a new transport hub for Lisbon in time for the World Expo in 1998. By creating a space that was a clear point of arrival, he aimed to inspire incoming visitors, and today the *Gare do Oriente* is set to become Lisbon's main transport hub when it undergoes a planned regeneration.

The main feature of the building is the interlocking white tree canopy made from steel and glass, which beautifully mimics shapes found in the natural world. The contrast of a naturalistic design constructed from man-made materials hints at Brutalism and is highly reminiscent of the ornamentation used in Gothic architecture. Taking this symbolism further, Calatrava favoured ramps and glass elevators over stairs, giving a sense of a natural incline within a forest.

Made from three self-contained parts and divided into two levels, operating both over and underground, the design was ambitious for its time and involved organizing several different modes of high-speed transport in one location. The folding geometric roof is 25m (82ft) high and each column was designed on a grid system alongside a main axis with five parallel rows of twinned concrete arches. One of the main reasons Calatrava won the bid was by linking two previously separated districts via an axis running between them, which transformed the project from simply a new transport hub into an urban planning project. Now known as one of Europe's most rational transport hubs, this modern take on Gothic architecture is a legacy of Expo 1998 that instils as much curiosity in the public today as when it was first built.

SCULPTURAL FORMS
Calatrava sculpts sweeping concave and convex lines into dramatic interiors made from sleek, naked materials.

KEY ARCHITECTURAL STYLES OF THE 21ST CENTURY

PASSIVHAUS (1990–PRESENT)

The first Passivhaus (or 'passive house') homes were constructed in Germany in 1990 and Passivhaus is now a model for constructing residential and commercial buildings that use very little energy to heat up and cool down. This is achieved in several ways, such as making the building airtight, using superinsulation, and installing advanced window technology and a ventilation system that delivers fresh air as a heat source. There are very strict requirements for a building to be classed as Passivhaus, and the construction process is more expensive due to the level of expertise required. However, the running cost of a Passivhaus building is minimal compared to regular builds and there are health benefits from circulating fresh air.

BIOMIMETIC (2006–PRESENT)

Biomimicry is an architectural philosophy that takes inspiration from qualities, processes, solutions and forms found in nature to create more effective and sustainable buildings. By understanding the ecosystemic rules that govern the forms, as well as the forms themselves, designers and architects can find innovative solutions to maximize performance, reduce maintenance and provide longer life cycles for buildings. Biomimicry looks at evolution and how problems have been solved by nature; for example, the water-repelling properties of a lotus leaf. By learning on a cellular level how the plant adapted to its environment, we can apply the same water-repelling techniques to surface finishes such as paints and renders for use in our built environment.

REINVENTION (1990–PRESENT)

Reinvention of existing architecture is a recent phenomenon that is at the forefront of development within the urban environment. It considers dilapidated and disused buildings and transforms them to fit the needs of new users and to breathe new life into degenerated urban areas. Its premise is that cities around the world already have many more structures than are actually required and there should be a focus on repurposing these, rather than adding more new buildings. With time, existing buildings have become useless as the functions of the building change, the way the space is used becomes dated or unfashionable and the advancement of digital technology has surpassed the buildings' functionality, making it more important than ever to reinvent them in order to create sustainable cities, minimize our waste and reduce our overall environmental impact.

MODERN ARAB ISLAMIC (1975–PRESENT)

Modern Islamic architecture features the traditional geometry used in ancient structures but with a contemporary twist; for example, by using a modern material and changing the scale and overall shape of the building. By taking a minimalist approach and using muted colours and tones, the form is celebrated, yet still alludes to its religious background. In recent times, with the aid of CAD (computer-aided design), larger and more articulated designs have become possible, displaying all the detail and intricacies of the ancient Islamic buildings, but with greater complexity and on a monumental scale.

21st-CENTURY ARCHITECTURE

We are now at a critical point in history, where sustainability and environmental concerns are shifting our political, social and economic priorities towards efforts to save the planet. The digital revolution and continuing advances in science and technology mean we live in an era of constant change, while concerns over global conflict and terrorism abide.

After the 9/11 attack on the United States in 2001, the ensuing 'War on Terror' led to military action and the devastation of large areas of the Middle East, some of which are currently being rebuilt. The 2004 Indian Ocean tsunami left more than 200,000 people dead and obliterated huge tracts of the coastlines of Indonesia, Thailand, Sri Lanka and India. Major development projects have since been launched to repair the damage done. The financial crisis of 2008 was considered to be the worst economic downturn since the Great Depression. Unemployment rose, house prices fell and stock markets suffered for several years. By the early 2010s, societal issues such as austerity, hate crime and identity politics led to public demonstrations and much media debate. Symbolically, the 2011 London riots, caused by increasing friction between inner-city youths and police, were superseded by the successful staging of the London Olympics the following year and the urban regeneration programmes that followed.

In creative terms, the development of technologies such as 3D printing made design more accessible than previously. For the building industry, the introduction of biomimicry allowed architects to look at how nature could assist them in their work.

TURNING TO NATURE
The Supertrees of Singapore offer a glimpse of what is possible using new technologies and innovative thinking.

PASSIVHAUS 1990–PRESENT

- Very **thick insulation**
- **Airtight** building
- Inbuilt **heat recovery** and ventilation systems
- **Goal** to achieve 90 per cent energy consumption reduction
- **Renewable** energy

THE ENTERPRISE CENTRE, UNIVERSITY OF EAST ANGLIA

Architect: Architype
Construction started: 2013
Construction completed: 2015
Construction materials: Timber, straw, hemp, clay, flint and structural glazing
Area: 3430sq m (36,920sq ft)
Location: Norwich, United Kingdom

The Enterprise Centre is one of the UK's most sustainable buildings and the first large commercial building in the UK to target and receive both Passivhaus certification and BREEAM (the world's leading sustainability assessment method) Outstanding rating – the two most difficult eco standards to meet for buildings. The main aim was to reduce greenhouse gas emissions from cradle to grave by producing a low-carbon building via a low-carbon construction process. Local products were central to the design, using building materials such as timber and hemp that were grown locally rather than processed and transported to site. 'Hempcrete', a combination of hemp and lime, replaced concrete; hemp was also used for walls due to its excellent insulation properties. The centre's façades are predominantly thatch prefabricated as cassettes locally for ease and future maintenance with reclaimed laboratory workbenches to form timber panels. This rethinking of building materials resulted in job creation and new start-up businesses, benefiting the local community at the same time as creating world-class innovative architecture.

The centre accommodates teaching and learning spaces alongside business and innovation tenants, creating dynamic interaction on multiple levels. Internally, wellbeing is at its heart, with interior spaces flooded with daylight and a focus on toxin-free materials. The use of recycled and natural materials results in minimal emissions and, as these are sourced locally, further reduces the building's footprint while also stimulating local small business. Cutting-edge technology and construction techniques also contributed to creating a building that achieves a sustainable reduction in emissions and represents an impressive new design vernacular.

HEMPCRETE
Hempcrete, or hemp mixed with lime, offers both excellent insulation properties and is acoustically successful in large open spaces. It is also a toxin-free material for use inside the building.

BIOMIMETIC 2006–PRESENT

- **Sustainable** design
- Simulation of the **natural world**
- **Investigates** the organism, its behaviours and the ecosystem it exists within
- Values **nature** as something we learn from

SUPERTREES, SINGAPORE

Architects: Wilkinson Eyre and Grant Associates
Construction started: 2007
Construction completed: 2012
Construction materials: Reinforced concrete, steel and plants
Height of tallest tree: 50m (160 ft)
Location: Marina South, Singapore

Biomimicry can be a simulation of the natural world; for example where a building 'repairs' itself as a living organism does. It can be seen in form, or in the copying of natural three-dimensional shapes. The 18 Supertrees of Singapore, which tower over its Gardens by the Bay nature park, fall into the second category. These giant structures were designed to mimic the form and function of mature trees and provide scale and a vertical dimension to the landscape and gardens they inhabit. They are constructed of reinforced concrete for vertical strength and wrapped in steel framing to provide planting support. Planting panels encase the tree trunk in a living 'skin' consisting of over 162,900 plants from more than 200 different species, creating beautiful displays of tropical flowering plants brought in from Brazil, Panama, Ecuador and Costa Rica. The Supertrees have different planting schemes in various colours, with plants chosen based on their suitability for vertical planting, being lightweight and hardy, soil-less and easy to maintain, as well as their suitability to the Singapore climate and their high visual interest.

Each Supertree has a large canopy shaped like an inverted umbrella and embedded with environmentally sustainable functions, such as photovoltaic cells to provide solar energy for lighting up the structure at night. They also act as air exhausts for the park's cooled conservatories and energy centre, and provide much-needed shade during the day. The Supertrees combine the appearance and some of the functions of natural trees with sustainable and cultural uses, creating a new man-made 'tree' used for a new purpose. The result is interesting architecture on a grand scale.

OCBC SKYWAY
This 128m-long (420ft) aerial walkway is 22m (72ft) off the ground and connects two Supertrees, offering close-up views of the Supertrees' canopy structures and their technology.

GARDENS BY THE BAY

A blend of nature, technology, environmental management and creativity form a 21st-century tropical horticulture and destination experience. The gardens include 18 Supertrees, a skyway, two giant cooled plant conservatories, and four heritage gardens with parkland and lakes, all linked with intelligent environmental infrastructure.

REINVENTION 1990–PRESENT

- **Sustainability**
- **Adapting** to new use and users
- Conserving and celebrating elements of **existing** buildings
- Using **holistic** design to reinvent

ZEITZ MUSEUM OF CONTEMPORARY ART AFRICA, CAPE TOWN

Architect: Heatherwick Studio
Construction started: 2014 (original structure built 1921, decommissioned 2001)
Construction completed: 2017
Construction materials: Concrete and glass
Height/Area: 57m (187ft) and 9500sq m (102,000sq ft)
Location: Cape Town, South Africa

The Zeitz Museum of Contemporary Art Africa (MOCAA) was a disused grain silo complex that stood as a monument to Cape Town's industrial past, and is still an instantly recognizable feature on the skyline of what is now the V&A Waterfront harbour area. The challenge was to create new from old without destroying the original building and to conserve and celebrate its original industrial heritage. Its transformation into the Zeitz MOCAA has breathed entirely new cultural life into the building, as well as creating an astounding piece of architecture.

The museum's 100 galleries and atrium space were carved out of the dense cellular concrete structure, consisting of 42 tubes spanning the entire 10-storey height of the building, to create an awe-inspiring interior atrium of monumental proportions with a cathedral-like quality. These enormous tubes had their concrete roofs removed, then openings were sliced into them and infilled with geometric convex windows modelled on Venetian blown glass lanterns, bathing the interior with sunlight and completely altering the perception of the space. The diamond-like windows add another dimension to the exterior, as they reflect light in different ways. Glass oval elevators slide up and down the carved concrete silo tubes, so visitors can be seen on varying levels moving between spaces. One can also stand on the bottom level of the museum and gaze skywards through dozens of sliced tubular volumes, providing a mesmerizing experience within a building that is in itself a sculptural artwork.

SILO CELLULAR STRUCTURE
The interior atrium is carved out of a dense cellular structure of 42 concrete tubes spanning the full height of the building, allowing daylight to transform the space.

MODERN ARAB ISLAMIC 1975–PRESENT

- Use of **domes** and **organic** shapes
- Ancient Islamic motifs **simplified** to contemporary shapes
- **Islamic** intricacies reinvented with modern materials
- **Peaceful**, quiet nature

LOUVRE ABU DHABI

Architect: Ateliers Jean Nouvel
Construction started: 2009
Construction completed: 2014
Construction materials: Steel, aluminium and fibre concrete
Height/Area: 40m (131ft) and 24,000sq m (260,000sq ft)
Location: Saadiyat Island, Abu Dhabi, United Arab Emirates

Louvre Abu Dhabi, a collaboration between the UAE and France to create a pioneering cultural landmark, was influenced by local traditional architectural culture and geographical context. It considered various Arabian and Islamic design intricacies and reinvented them to suit modern materials and provide contemporary design solutions. Referencing traditional low-lying Arab settlements, a series of 55 individual white buildings clad in high-performance fibre concrete make up the museum. These buildings are sheltered by the awe-inspiring 180m-diameter (590ft) dome, a traditional symbol of Islamic architecture, which in this case is flattened to provide perfectly radiating geometry and covered with a perforated material, resulting in a modern reinvention of a traditional form. The dome consists of a complex pattern of steel and aluminium stars of varying sizes that tesselate over eight layers to create a roof structure that seems to magically float on air. Around 8000 patterned perforations in the roof also bring in a dappled light that changes throughout the day.

Elsewhere, the use of water has been taken to a different technological level. A heavily engineered, watertight basement structure was designed to allow for tidal pools around the galleries, giving the illusion of a building at sea. Louvre Abu Dhabi illustrates how traditional design and modern construction techniques can work together in an attempt to bridge the gap between culture and technology. The museum relates to the country's history, geography, religion and culture without becoming a direct translation of traditional architecture. It creates tranquillity through complexity of design, a characteristic seen in traditional Islamic architecture and successfully translated to this contemporary structure.

SHADED WALKWAYS
Contemporary geometric white lattice walkways provide dappled shade, while linking structures together and addressing the entrance to the main building.

RAIN OF LIGHT (ABOVE)
Almost 8000 star-patterned perforations layered across the dome bring in dappled sunlight, with each ray of the sun creating shifting shadows throughout the museum.

GRAND VESTIBULE (LEFT)
This room acts as an introduction to the rest of the museum. It is flooded with light and draws one's attention to the floor, which is covered in marine charts of the area.

DOME (FAR LEFT)
The geometric roof structure is made up from various sized and angled stars, intertwined into a total of eight layers of cladding. The four outer layers are stainless steel and the four inner are aluminium. The largest star is 13m (47ft) in diameter and weighs 1.3 tonnes (1.2 tons).

GLOSSARY

Apse
Semicircular or polygonal end of a church; usually the end of the chancel, at the east end.

Balusters
Small pillar or column supporting rail.

Buttress
Reinforced, projecting wall, usually on the exterior of a building, supporting it at a point of stress. A flying buttress transmits the thrust of a vault to an outer support.

Caryatid
A column that takes the form of a standing female figure.

Chancel
East end of church containing the altar.

Chhatri
Elevated, dome-shaped pavilion used as an element in Indian architecture.

Ciborium
Free-standing canopy, originally fabric, over an altar.

Cornice
Derived from the Italian word meaning 'ledge', a cornice refers to any horizontal, decorative moulding that crowns a building.

Cruck frame
A curved timber frame, one of a pair, which supports the roof of a building.

Dentils
Small rectangular blocks that, when placed together in a row abutting a moulding, suggest a row of teeth.

Entablature
A horizontal part in classical architecture that rests on the columns and consists of architrave, frieze and cornice.

Frieze
A band of richly sculpted ornamentation on a building.

Gambrel roof
Ridged roof with two slopes at each side, the lower slopes being steeper than the upper slopes.

Iconostasis
The vertical element commonly found in the altar area of Christian Orthodox churches and Eastern Catholic churches, on which several religious figures are represented.

Lintel
A structural horizontal support used to span an opening in a wall or between two vertical supports. It is frequently used over windows and doors.

Mihrab
A wall recess, mostly in the form of arched niche, in the *qibla* wall. It indicates the direction of Mecca.

Mullions
A structural unit that divides adjacent windows.

Muqarnas
A three-dimensional decoration of Islamic architecture typically applied to the undersides of domes, pendentives, cornices, squinches, arches and vaults and often seen in the *mihrab* of a mosque.

Orders of architecture
The three primary orders of Classical architecture, used in ancient Greece and ancient Rome are, chronologically: the Doric order, the Ionic order and the Corinthian order.

Ogee arch
Arch consisting of two opposing 'S' curves meeting in a point at the apex.

Pendentive dome
A constructive device permitting the placing of a circular dome over a square room or an elliptical dome over a rectangular room.

Peristyle
Colonnade around a Classical temple or court, or an inner court in a large house surrounded by a colonnade.

Pietra dura
The inlay technique of using cut and fitted, highly polished coloured stones to create images.

Pilaster
Rectangular attached column that projects from a wall by less than one third of its width.

Portico
An entrance porch with columns or pilasters and a roof, and often crowned by a triangular pediment.

Qibla
The direction of Mecca, which Muslims should face while praying.

Quoin
Large stone or block laid at the corner of a building (or at an opening) used either for reinforcement of the angle or for ornament.

Spandrel
The roughly triangular space or surface that is found between a curved figure and a rectangular boundary.

Squinch
A straight or arched structure across an interior angle of a square tower to carry a superstructure such as a dome.

Transept
In a church, the arm that crosses the nave at right angles, usually separating it from the apse; twin transept arms may also project from the nave without interrupting it.

Triforium
Arcaded wall passage in a Gothic nave wall, between the clerestory and the main arcade in a three-storey elevation; in a four-storey elevation, it appears between the gallery and the clerstory.

Tympanum
The semicircular or triangular decorative wall surface over an entrance, door or window, which is bounded by a lintel and arch.

INDEX

References to images are in *italics*.

Acropolis, Athens 20–3
Africa:
   Fiat Tagliero Service Station, Asmara 160–1
   Zeitz Museum of Contemporary Art Africa, Cape Town 214–15
Alexander the Great 13
Alhambra, Granada 36–9
altars 67, *68*
Aman, Johan 95
Amenhotep III, Pharoah 13
American Colonial architecture 100, 104–5
Ancient Egyptian architecture 8, 9, 12–15
Ancient Greek architecture 8, 20–3
Ancient Roman architecture 8, 9, 24–7
Anne, Queen 100
Anne of Denmark 89
Anne Hathaway's Cottage, Stratford-upon-Avon 64–5
Anthemius of Tralles 33
arches 25, 31, 80, 93
   Fascist 163
   Leaning Tower of Pisa 43
   Norwich Cathedral 45
   Notre-Dame 49
   Saint Demetrius 41
   Taj Mahal *81*
Art Deco architecture 148, 156–9, 161
Art Nouveau architecture 126, 136–9
Arts and Crafts architecture 126, 140–1
Assyrian architecture 8, 18–19
Athena 21, *22*
atriums *177*, *195*, 199, 215
Austria 94–5, 101

balconies 119
Baroque architecture 80, 82–5, 100
bas-relief work 113
Bauhaus architecture 148, 152–5
Bauhaus, Dessau 152–5
Beaux-Arts architecture 126, 130–1
Belgium: Church of Saint Peter and Saint Paul, Ostend 114–17
Berlin Philharmonie 172–5
Biomimetic architecture 206
   Supertrees, Singapore *207*, 210–13
Bluecoat Chambers, Liverpool 106–7
Boitaca, Diogo de 67
Bramante, Donato 71
Brazil 178, 190–1
brickwork 47, 65; *see also* red brick
British Regency architecture 126, 128–9
bronze 183
Brunelleschi, Filippo 61
Brutalism 148, 169, 177, 178, 201, 205
   Cité Radieuse, Marseille *149*, 170–1
Bulfinch, Charles 121

Burghley House, Stamford 78–9
burial sites 31, *69*
   Taj Mahal, Agra *81*, 96–9
   Tomb of the Samanids, Bukhara 30–1
Byzantine architecture 28, 30–5

Cai Xin 53
Calatrava, Santiago 178, 204–5
Callicrates 21
calligraphic inscriptions 28, 37
Cambio, Arnolfo di 61
carvings 13, 17, 19, 41, 67, 87
   Forbidden City, Beijing *55*
   Hagia Sophia 33
   Leaning Tower of Pisa 43
   Notre-Dame, Paris 49
cathedrals:
   Cathedral of Brasília 190–1
   Florence 60–3
   Norwich *29*, 44–5
   Notre-Dame, Paris 48–51
   Saint Basil's, Moscow 74–7
   Saint Demetrius, Vladimir 40–1
   Vilnius *101*, 112–13
   see also churches
Cecil, Robert 87
Cecil, William 79
ceilings 87, 95, *144*, 201
   rib-vaulted 45, 67, *135*
chapels 103
   King's College Chapel, Cambridge 56–7
Charles I, King 81
Charles VI, Emperor 95
chhatris 97
Chichen Itza *6*, 9, 16–17
China 28, 29
   Forbidden City, Beijing 52–5
   Suzhou Museum 188–9
Chrysler Building, New York 156–9
churches 28
   Church of Saint Peter and Saint Paul, Ostend 114–17
   Church of the Intercession at Fili, Moscow 92–3
   Hagia Sophia, Istanbul 32–5
   Sagrada Família, Barcelona *127*, 142–5
   see also chapels
Circus, The, Bath 108–11
Cité Radieuse, Marseille *149*, 170–1
class 29, 151
Classical architecture 25, 58, 61, *62*, 80
   Beaux-Arts 131
   British Regency 129
   Federal style 121
   Georgian architecture 109
   Jeffersonian architecture 123, *124–5*
   Le Corbusier 185
   Palazzo Te, Mantua 73

   Queen's House, Greenwich 89
   Tempietto, Rome 71
   see also Neoclassical architecture
Clerk, Simon 57
cloisters 45, 67
Clough, George Albert 105
colonnades *90*, 129
Colosseum, Rome 24–7
colour 143, 151
columns 13, 15, 21, 43, 67, 129
concrete 148, 153, 171, 185
Corinthian architecture 8, 21, 25, 109
Costa, Veríssimo da 119
courtyards 37, 79
Crater Lake Lodge 146–7
curtain walling 153, 167, 183

David, King 73
deconstructivism 192–3
Delacenserie, Louis 115
dentil cornices 109, 121, 133
Diotisalvi 43
domes 28, 31, 71, 97, 123
   Florence Cathedral 61, *63*
   Hagia Sophia 33, *35*
   Louvre Abu Dhabi 217, *218*
   onion 75, *76*, 93
Doric architecture 8, 21, 25, 71, 105, 109

École des Beaux-Arts 126, 131
Edwardian architecture 148, 150–1
Egypt 8, 9, 12–15, 157
elevators 157
Elizabethan architecture 58, 78–9
Ely, Reginald 57
England 28, 29, 80, 81, 101
   Anne Hathaway's Cottage, Stratford-upon-Avon 64–5
   Bluecoat Chambers, Liverpool 106–7
   Burghley House, Stamford 78–9
   Circus, The, Bath 108–11
   Enterprise Centre, University of East Anglia 208–9
   Hatfield House 86–7
   King's College Chapel, Cambridge 56–7
   Lloyd's Building, London 176–7
   London Aquatics Centre 200–3
   Manchester Town Hall 132–5
   Moseley Road Baths, Birmingham 150–1
   Norwich Cathedral *29*, 44–5
   Park Crescent, London 128–9
   Queen's House, Greenwich 88–91
   Red House, Bexleyheath 140–1
   St Mary Axe, London 198–9
Enterprise Centre, University of East Anglia 208–9
environment, the 179, 199, 209
Eritrea 161

Fascist architecture 148, 162–3
Federal architecture 100, 120–1
Fiat Tagliero Service Station, Asmara 160–1
Fischer von Erlach, Johann Bernard 95
Florence Cathedral 60–3
flying buttresses 49, *51*
Fontana, Giovanni Mario 103
Forbidden City, Beijing 52–5
fortresses 19, 36–9
Foster, Norman 148, 178, 198–9
France 80, 81, 101, 126, 127, 148, 178
    Cité Radieuse, Marseille *149*, 170–1
    Notre-Dame Cathedral, Paris 48–51
    Palace of Versailles 82–5
    Saint Geneviève Library, Paris 130–1
    Villa Savoye, Poissy 184–7
frescoes 41, *59*, *63*, *73*, *83*, *93*, 95
Futurist architecture 148, 149, 160–1, 192–3, 201

gables 65, 87, 105, 121
gardens 83, *85*, 95, 141, 189
gargoyles 49, 157, *158*
gateways 79, 97
Gaudí, Antonio 126, *127*, 142–5
Gehry, Frank O. *7*, 178, 192–5
geometric patterns 28, 109, 157, 165, 167
    Le Corbusier 185
    Niemeyer 191
Georgian architecture 100, 105, 108–11, 121
Germany:
    Bauhaus, Dessau 152–5
    Berlin Philharmonic 172–5
'Gherkin, The' see St Mary Axe, London
glass 173, 177, 199
Gonzaga, Eleonora von 95
Gothic architecture 28, 48–51, 133, 141, 169, 205; see also Gothic Revival architecture; Perpendicular Gothic architecture
Gothic Revival architecture 100, 114–17
Graham, Bruce 167
Grand Menshikov Palace, Oranienbaum 102–3
Great Britain 127; see also England
Greece 8, 20–3
grid plans 119
Gropius, Walter 153
Gucevičius, Laurynas 113
Guerrini, Giovanni 163
Guggenheim Museum, Bilbao *7*, 192–5
Guglielmo 43

Hadid, Zaha 178, 179, 200–3
Hagia Sophia, Istanbul 32–5
Hale, William 151
Hardouin-Mansart, Jules 83
Hatfield House 86–7
Hathaway, Anne 65
heating 65, 133, 151, 177, 206, 209
Hempcrete 209
Henry IV, King 81

Henry VIII, King 59
High Renaissance architecture 58, 70–1
High Tech architecture 148, 176–7
Hitler, Adolf 148
Horemheb 13
housing:
    Anne Hathaway's Cottage, Stratford-upon-Avon 64–5
    Bauhaus, Dessau 152–5
    Burghley House, Stamford 78–9
    Circus, The, Bath 108–11
    Cité Radieuse, Marseille *149*, 170–1
    Crater Lake Lodge 146–7
    Hatfield 86–7
    Monticello, Charlottesville 122–5
    Park Crescent, London 128–9
    Passivhaus 206
    Queen's House, Greenwich 88–91
    Red House, Bexleyheath 140–1
    Taliesin West, Scottsdale 180–1
    Villa Savoye, Poissy 184–7
    see also 'prodigy houses'
Hungary: Museum of Applied Arts, Budapest 136–9

Iktinus 21
Imhotep 9
India 80, 81, 137–9
    Taj Mahal, Agra 96–9
insulation 206, 209
International Style 148, 166–7, 178, 189
Ionic architecture 8, 21, 107, 109, 129
Iraq 8, 9
    Palace of Sargon at Khorsabad 18–19
    Ziggurat of Ur 11
ironwork 131
Isidore of Miletus 33
Islamic architecture 28, 30–1, 206, 216–19; see also Moorish architecture; Mudéjar architecture; Mughal architecture
Ismail Samani 31
Italy 8, 9, 59, 80, 161
    Colosseum, Rome 24–7
    Florence Cathedral 60–3
    Leaning Tower of Pisa 42–3
    Palazzo della Civiltà Italiana, Rome 162–3
    Palazzo Ducale, Florence *59*
    Palazzo Te, Mantua 72–3
    Tempietto, Rome 70–1
Ivan the Terrible 75

Jacobean architecture 80, 86–7
James I, King 80, 89
Jefferson, Thomas 100, 123
Jeffersonian architecture 100, 122–5
Jones, Inigo 80, 89

Khan, Fazlur Rahman 167
King's College Chapel, Cambridge 56–7
Kuai Xiang 53

La Padula, Ernest Bruno 163
Labrouste, Henri 131

Lahauri, Ustad Ahmad 97
Late Musovite architecture 80, 92–3
Le Corbusier 148, 171, 178, 179, 184–7
Le Vau, Louis 83
Leaning Tower of Pisa 42–3
Lechner, Ödön 137
Leopold I, Emperor 95
light 143, 197
lighting 133, 157
limestone 17, 25
Lisbon Oriente Station 204–5
Litherland, Edward 107
Lithuania: Vilnius Cathedral *101*, 112–13
Llobregat Sports Centre, Barcelona 196–7
Lloyd's Building, London 176–7
local material 126, 147, 209
loggias 73, 87, 89
London Aquatics Centre 200–3
Louis XIII, King 81, 83
Louis XIV, King 81, 83
Louvre Abu Dhabi 216–19
Luxor Temple 12–15

McIntire, Samuel 121
Manchester Town Hall 132–5
Mannerism architecture 58, 72–3
Manuel I, King 58, 59
Manueline architecture 58, 66–9
Maria Theresa, Empress 95
Marinetti, Filippo Tommaso 148
Mayans 17
Medieval Rus' architecture 28, 40–1
Menshikov, Prince 103
Mesoamerican architecture 6, 8, 9, 16–17
Mexico 8
    Chichen Itza *6*, 9, 16–17
Michelangelo 80
Middle Musovite architecture 58, 74–7
Mies van der Rohe, Ludwig 178, 182–3
minarets 97
Ming China architecture 28, 29, 52–5
minimalism 153, 157, 163, 201, 205
mirrors 80, 83, *84*
Mnesikles 21
Modern Islamic architecture 206, 216–19
Modernism *7*, 179, 182–7, 189; see also Postmodernism
monasteries: Santa Cruz, Coimbra 66–9
Monticello, Charlottesville 122–5
Moorish architecture 28, 36–9
Morris, William 141
mosaics 33, 137
Moscow State University 168–9
Moseley Road Baths, Birmingham 150–1
Mudéjar architecture 28, 46–7
Mughal architecture 80, 96–9, 137–9
Mumtaz Mahal 97
Museum of Applied Arts, Budapest 136–9
museums:
    Guggenheim Museum, Bilbao *7*, 192–5
    Louvre Abu Dhabi 216–19
    Museum of Applied Arts, Budapest 136–9

New Mexico Museum of Art, Santa Fe 164–5
Suzhou Museum 188–9
Zeitz Museum of Contemporary Art Africa, Cape Town 214–15
Mussolini, Benito 148, 161, 163

Nabonidus, King 11
Napoleonic Wars 127
Nash, John 129
Native Americans 148, 165
nature 179, 181, 205, 206, 211
naves *29, 50, 68*
Nebuchadnessar II, King 11
Neoclassical architecture 100, *101*, 112–13, 119
New Mexico Museum of Art, Santa Fe 164–5
Nguyen An 53
Niemeyer, Oscar 178, 190–1
Norman architecture 28, 29, 44–5
Norwich Cathedral, England *29*, 44–5
Notre-Dame Cathedral, Paris 48–51

Old State House, Boston 104–5
Old Town Hall, Salem 120–1

paintings *77, 79, 98*; see also frescoes; murals
palaces:
    Forbidden City, Beijing 52–5
    Grand Menshikov Palace, Oranienbaum 102–3
    Palace of Versailles 82–5
    Palazzo Ducale, Florence *59*
    Palazzo Te, Mantua 72–3
    Sargon at Khorsabad 18–19
    Schönbrunn Palace 94–5
Palazzo della Civiltà Italiana, Rome 162–3
Palladian architecture 80, 88–91, 113
Palladio, Andrea 6, 80, 123
Park Crescent, London 128–9
Parkitecture 126, 146–7
Parthenon 21, *22*
Pártos, Gyula 137
Pascassi, Nikolaus 95
Passivhaus architecture 206, 208–9
pavilions 103
Pei, I.M. 178, 188–9
Perpendicular Gothic architecture 28, 56–7
Persian architecture 28, 29, 30–1
Peter, St 71
Peter the Great 81, 100, 101
Petrine Baroque architecture 100, 102–3
Pettazzi, Giuseppe 161
Phidias 21
pinwheel layout 153, *154*
Pires, Marcos 67
Pisano, Bonanno & Tommaso 43
Pombaline Style architecture 100, 118–19
Portugal 58, 59, 100, 178
    Lisbon Oriente Station 204–5
    Praça do Comércio, Lisbon 118–19
    Santa Cruz Monastery, Coimbra 66–9
Postmodern architecture 148, 172–5, 177

Praça do Comércio, Lisbon 118–19
'prodigy houses' 58, 79, 80
public buildings:
    Bauhaus, Dessau 152–5
    Berlin Philharmonic 172–5
    Bluecoat Chambers, Liverpool 106–7
    Enterprise Centre, University of East Anglia 208–9
    Fiat Tagliero Service Station, Asmara 160–1
    Lisbon Oriente Station 204–5
    Manchester Town Hall 132–5
    Old State House, Boston 104–5
    Old Town Hall, Salem 120–1
    Palazzo della Civiltà Italiana, Rome 162–3
    Saint Geneviève Library, Paris 130–1
    see also museums; sports centres and swimming pools
Pueblo Revival architecture 148, 164–5
pyramids 9, 11, 17

Queen Anne architecture 100, 106–7
Queen's House, Greenwich 88–91

Ramses II, Pharoah 13, 15
Rapp, Isaac 165
Rastrelli, Francesco Bartolomeo 103
red brick *47, 75, 87, 93, 123*, 141, 151
Red House, Bexleyheath 140–1
Reinvention architecture 206, 214–15
relief work 43, 95, 113
Renaissance architecture 58, 60–3; see also High Renaissance architecture
Rinaldi, Antonio 103
Rococo architecture 80, 94–5
Rogers, Isaiah 105
Rogers, Richard 148, 177
Roman Empire 8, 9, 24–7, 29
Romanesque architecture 28, 29, 41, 42–3
Romano, Giulio 73, 80
Romano, Mario 163
roofs *54*, 83, 87, 133, *202*
Rudnev, Lev 169
Russia 28, 59, 80, 81, 100, 101
    Cathedral of Saint Demetrius, Vladimir 40–1
    Church of the Intercession at Fili, Moscow 92–3
    Grand Menshikov Palace, Oranienbaum 102–3
    Moscow State University 168–9
    Saint Basil's Cathedral, Moscow 74–7
    Stalinist architecture 148

Sagrada Familia, Barcelona *127*, 142–5
Saint Basil's Cathedral, Moscow 74–7
Saint Geneviève Library, Paris 130–1
St Mary Axe, London 198–9
Salvin, Anthony 45
San Martin Tower, Teruel 46–7
Sancho I, King 69
Santa Cruz Monastery, Coimbra 66–9
Santos, Eugénio dos 119
Sargon II, King 19
Schädel, Gottfried 103

Scharoun, Hans 173
Schönbrunn Palace 94–5
science 127, 149, 207
sculpture *135*, 143
Seagram Building, New York 182–3
Shah Jahan 97
Singapore: Supertrees *207*, 210–13
Siza, Álvaro 178, 196–7
skyscrapers:
    Chrysler Building, New York 156–9
    Moscow State University 168–9
    Seagram Building, New York 182–3
    St Mary Axe, London 198–9
    Supertrees, Singapore *207*, 210–13
    Willis Tower, Chicago 166–7
Soviet Union see Russia
Spain 127
    Alhambra, Granada 36–9
    Guggenheim Museum, Bilbao *7*, 192–5
    Llobregat Sports Centre, Barcelona 196–7
    Sagrada Familia, Barcelona *127*, 142–5
    San Martin Tower, Teruel 46–7
sports centres and swimming pools:
    Llobregat Sports Centre, Barcelona 196–7
    London Aquatics Centre 200–3
    Moseley Road Baths, Birmingham 150–1
stained-glass 45, 57, 143, *145*, 191
stainless steel 157, 177
staircases 87, 89, 105, 141, 171
    Bauhaus *154*
    Le Corbusier *186*
    Manchester Town Hall *134*
Stalinist architecture 148, 168–9
Steers, Thomas 107
streets and squares:
    Circus, The, Bath 108–11
    Park Crescent, London 128–9
    Praça do Comércio, Lisbon 118–19
Sully, Maurice de 49
Sumerian architecture 8, 9, 10–11
Supertrees, Singapore *207*
sustainability 206, 209, 211, 215
Suzhou Museum 188–9

Taj Mahal, Agra *81*, 96–9
Taliesin West, Scottsdale 180–1
technology 127, 137, 149, 161, 167, 206, 207
Tempietto, Rome 70–1
temples 8, 10–11, 12–15, 19, 21, 70–1
tiles *47, 54, 67*, 137
timber frame construction 58, 65, 75
titanium 193
Titus, Emperor 25
Tomb of the Samanids, Bukhara 30–1
towers 28, 42–3, 46–7, 161; see also skyscrapers
Tudor, House of 58, 59
Turkey: Hagia Sophia, Istanbul 32–5
Tutankhamun, Pharoah 13

United Arab Emirates: Louvre Abu Dhabi 216–19

United States of America 100, 101, 126, 148, 178
   Chrysler Building, New Yok 156–9
   Crater Lake Lodge 146–7
   Monticello, Charlottesville 122–5
   New Mexico Museum of Art, Santa Fe 164–5
   Old State House, Boston 104–5
   Old Town Hall, Salem 120–1
   Seagram Building, New York 182–3
   Taliesin West, Scottsdale 180–1
   Willis Tower, Chicago 166–7
Uzbekistan: Tomb of the Samanids, Bukhara 30–1

Van Alen, William 157
vaulting *29*, 57
ventilation 123, 133, 153, 181, *177*, 199, 206
Vernacular Tudor architecture 58, 64–5
Vespasian, Emperor 25
Victorian architecture 126, 132–5
Villa Savoye, Poissy 184–7
Vilnius Cathedral *101*, 112–13

Wastell, John 57
Waterhouse, Alfred 133
Webb, Philip 141
Willis Tower, Chicago 166–7
windows 37, 49, 57, 71, *117*, 123
   Bauhaus 153
   bull's eye 107
   casement 65
   mullioned 87
   ribbon 185
   rose 61
   sash 105
   see also stained-glass
Wood the Elder & Younger, John 109
Woolley, Sir Leonard 11
Wright, Frank Lloyd 178, 179, 180–1, 193
wrought iron 131

Yakovlev, Postnik 75

Zeitz Museum of Contemporary Art Africa, Cape Town 214–15
Ziggurat of Ur 11

PICTURE CREDITS

Alamy: 6 (Graham Mulrooney), 7 (Arcaid), 10 (Nik Wheeler), 11 (Robert Harding), 16 (Russell Mills Travel), 23 & 24 (Funkyfood London/Paul Williams), 26/27 (Stanislav Halcin), 31 (Image Leaks), 34 (Michele Burgess), 36 (Mauritius Images), 37 (Museo Pics/Paul Williams), 44 (Karen Fuller), 45 (Chris Herring), 46 (Stefano Politi Markovina), 47 (Marcos Veiga), 51 (Tom Corban), 52 & 54 bottom (Prisma by Dukas Presseagentur), 53 (AvadaRM), 55 (Robert Harding), 56 (J L Images), 60 (Grant Rooney Premium), 63 (Mark Beton), 64 (Greg Balfour Evans), 72 (S Forster), 76 (Robert Harding/Richard Maschmeyer), 81 (Michele Burgess), 85 (Moonie's World Photography), 86 (Robert Wyatt), 87 (Tony French), 90 top (Image Broker), 90 bottom (Steve Vidler), 91 (Angelo Hornak), 93 (Ivan Vdovin), 99 top (Look Die Bildagentur der Fotografen), 99 bottom (Dinodia Photos), 105 (Susan Candelario), 107 (Andy Marshall), 109 (Colin Underhill), 110/111 (A M Stock2), 113 (Timothy Mulholland), 114 (Brent Beach), 120 (Steven Milne), 121 (Richard Cummins), 122 (Washington Imaging), 123 (Purestock), 124 (David Struckel), 125 (Evan Sklar), 128 (Simon Hart), 129 (Mal Smith), 130 (Glenn Harper), 131 (Hemis), 132 (Martin Priestley), 133 (Mark Waugh), 135 top (Craig Travis), 137 (Travel Collection), 140 & 141 (Bildarchiv Monheim), 142 (John Kellerman), 144 (Hemis), 147 (Blend Images), 149 (Chris Hellier), 150 (Arcaid), 151 (Simon Webster), 156 (Inge Johnson), 158 top (Travelpix), 159 (Martin Cameron), 160 (Robert Harding), 161 (Eric Lafforgue), 163 (Massimo Lama), 164 (Allen Russell), 165 (Craig Lovell/Eagle Visions Photography), 166 (Chuck Place), 167 (Andy Guest), 169 (De Rocker), 170 (Geoffrey Taunton), 171 (Chris Hellier), 172 (Eye Ubiquitous), 173 (Ingo Jezierski), 176 (Mark Richardson), 180 (Stephen Saks Photography), 181 (Elizabeth Holmes), 182 (Thomas Lee), 184 & 185 (Bildarchiv Mondheim), 186 (B O'Kane), 187 top (Arcaid), 187 bottom (Arcaid/Valeria Carullo), 188 & 189 (Michael Freeman), 192 (Eye Ubiquitous/Michael Lee), 194 (Peter Domotor), 197 (Arcaid), 199 (Prixpics), 204 (Image Broker/Stefan Kiever), 208 & 209 (View/Dennis Gilbert), 216 & 218 (Hemis/Franck Guiziou)

Dreamstime: 5 (Alexandre Fagundes De Fagundes), 22 (Paule Marjanovic), 29 (Steve Allen), 30 (Edmongin), 42 (Krisztian Miklosy), 48 (Vladislav Gajic), 49 (Tom Corban), 50 (Orionna), 51 (Johnypan), 54 top (Pixattitude), 59 (Veronica Antonello), 61 & 62 top (Bob Hilscher), 62 bottom (Inna Felker), 65 (Altosan), 70 & 71 (Stefano Valeri), 73 (Wieslaw Jarek), 92 (Viacheslav Silantev), 108 (Christophe Capelli), 136 (Romasph), 145 bottom (Thvirex), 152 & 154 top (Jacek Kadaj), 174 top (Vasilii Maslak), 177 (Philip Bird), 190 (Felipe Frazao), 191 (Bevanward), 193 & 195 (Karol Kozlowski), 205 (Saiko3p), 211 (Svetlana Day), 217 (Kentu Saarits)

FLPA: 15 (Reinhard Dirscherl)

Getty Images: 12 (Robert Harding/Philip Craven), 13 (National Geographic/Richard Nowitz), 14 (Moment/Angel Villalba), 18 & 19 (De Agostini/Dagli Orti), 20 (Photolibrary/Australian Scenics), 68 (Tony Eggers), 78 (Visit Britain/Dave Porter), 88 (Universal Images Group/View Pictures), 94 (Imagno), 106 (Mark Sykes), 116 (Moment/Philippe Debled), 134 (AWL Images/Mark Sykes), 135 bottom (Epics), 146 (George Rose), 157 (Nathan Benn), 158 bottom (Pete Seward Photography), 162 (Vincenzo Lombardo), 183 (James Leynse), 196 (View Pictures), 198 (Photographer's Choice/Andy Holt), 214 (Westend 61), 219 (Tom Dulat)

iStock: 104 (400tmax)

Shutterstock: 9 (Anton Ivano), 15 top (Sylwia Ciesielski), 17 (Fstop101), 21 (Cliomiu), 25 (Nakarin), 32 (Muratart), 33 (Steve Lovegoave), 36 (Mikhail Markovskiy), 38/39 (Tom Roche), 40 (Tousla), 41 (Grigory Lugovoy), 43 (Lucag_g), 57 (David Young), 66 (Saiko 3p), 67 & 69 (Vladmir Korostyshevskiy), 74 (Kostin SS), 75 (Millionstock), 77 top (Natalia Volkova), 77 bottom (Xabi Kis), 79 (Trabantos), 82 (Andre Quinov), 83 (Felix Lipov), 84 (Mister Knight), 89 (Philip Reeve), 95 (Dundanim), 96 (Turtix), 97 (Ankit M), 98 (Igor Dymov), 101 (Ppictures), 102 (Inna Poka), 103 (LLady Jane), 112 (Agne Svagzdyte), 115 (Gudok Mari), 117 (Stas Knop), 118 (T T Studio), 119 (Archiwiz), 127 (Anastasios 71), 138 & 139 (Acbareva), 143 (Anna Bogush), 145 top (Aleksandar Mijatovic), 153 & 154 bottom (Claudio Divizia), 155 (Urbanoid Pro), 168 (Marco Rubino), 174 bottom & 175 (Posztos), 179 (Pio3), 200 (Ron Ellis), 201 (Neil Laing), 202 (eXpose), 203 (Mitch Gunn), 206 (Littleaom), 210 (Carlotta Menna), 212/213 (Joyfull), 215 (Christianthiel.net), 219 top (Smoxx)